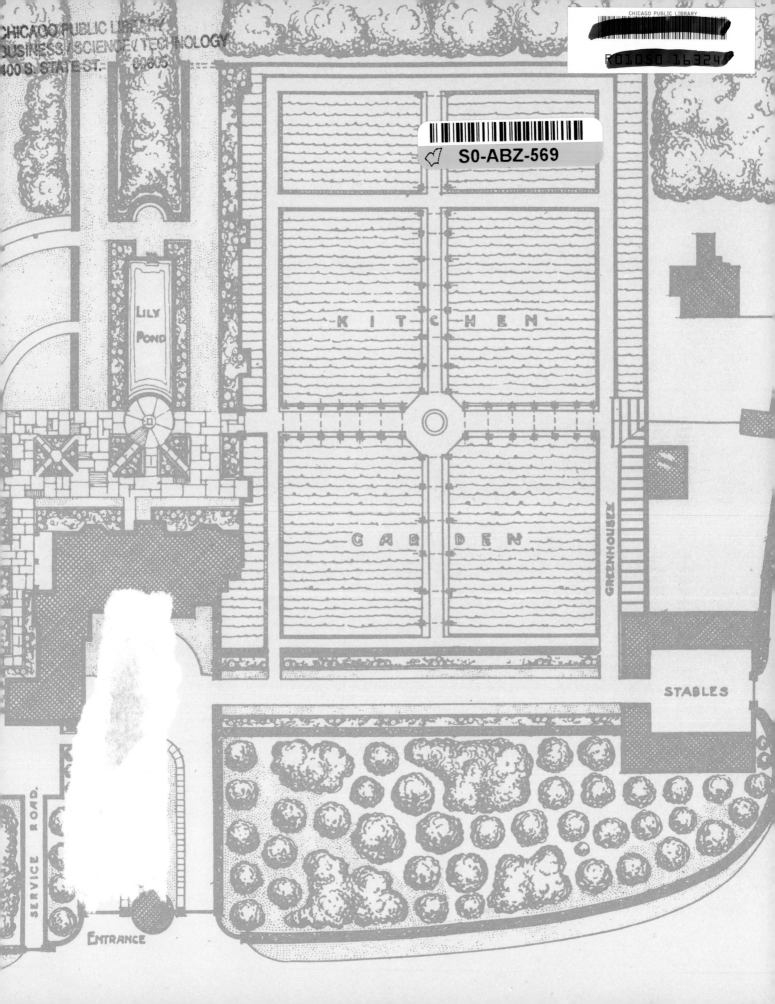

S0-ABZ-569

LILY POND

KITCHEN

GARDEN

GREENHOUSE

STABLES

SERVICE ROAD.

Entrance

GREAT
GARDENS
GREAT
DESIGNERS

GREAT
GARDENS
GREAT
DESIGNERS

GEORGE PLUMPTRE

WARD LOCK

A Ward Lock Book

First published in the UK 1994
by Ward Lock
Villiers House, 41/47 Strand
LONDON WC2N 5JE

A Cassell Imprint

Distributed in the United States
by Sterling Publishing Co., Inc.
387 Park Avenue South, New York,
NY 10016-8810

Distributed in Australia
by Capricorn Link (Australia) Pty Ltd
2/13 Carrington Road, Castle Hill NSW 2154

A British Library Cataloguing in Publication Data
block for this book may be obtained from the
British Library

ISBN 0 7063 7203 4

House Editor: Stuart Cooper
Project Editor: Alison Wormleighton
Designer: Ronald Clark
Picture Researcher: Julia Pashley

Typeset by Litho Link Ltd, Welshpool, Powys
Printed and bound in Spain by Cronion S.A., Barcelona.

(*Half-title page*) At Hestercombe a classical stone wall mask
spouting water exemplifies Edwin Lutyens's architectural detail.

(*Frontispiece*) Buscot Park, Oxfordshire, where Harold Peto's
designs of formal water features harmonize with the classical
architecture.

Contents

Part III – THE ESSENCE OF GOOD GARDEN DESIGN

A delicate wrought-iron gateway at Heale House, Wiltshire,
a garden designed by Harold Peto.

Introduction

Garden design can appear a mystery, a labyrinth of high-sounding theories about architecture and planting, garden ornaments and water: easily admired but difficult to understand. *Great Gardens, Great Designers* sets out to make this fascinating subject accessible and relevant. Discussing the work of a selection of highly influential designers and plantsmen whose work has been of fundamental importance through the 20th century, the book reveals the different elements and priorities of their work in a combination of text, photographs and plans. It is selective, not comprehensive, and clearly focuses on the principal developments.

The book begins by describing how the end of the 19th century was a watershed in the development of garden design. The lavish Victorian garden became something to react against. Out of this came the Arts and Crafts movement, and the aspiration for a human element which has continued throughout the 20th century. Although garden designs of the 1890s may now seem historically far removed, the details of the great designers' work, and their guiding beliefs, are in fact still enormously relevant.

The book also shows how, as the 20th century progressed, the variety of ideas about what is acceptable and fashionable in garden design has expanded to a far greater extent than during any previous period. While these ideas continue to be applied to the kind of expansive gardens which characterized the past, design has now also become increasingly important for small gardens, be they in town or country.

Great Gardens, Great Designers clearly explains in three separate but closely related sections how there has been a thread of continuity through the 20th-century garden, from the Arts and Crafts movement to the present day. Part I describes the principles of Arts and Crafts and its impact on gardens, before relating the ideas used by the century's main designers. In Part II individual gardens of these designers are discussed, highlighting the qualities of their work and how they are adaptable. And Part III discusses a selection of garden design themes such as border planting, the use of ornament, and designing a small garden.

The designers included have worked in both Britain and the United States. Many have also worked in other countries but the text deliberately confines itself to their Anglo-American projects to avoid presenting too complex a picture. The reader will be able to appreciate the manner in which British styles have influenced American gardens, and how the reverse has also been true.

Throughout the book the different designers are frequently quoted, so bringing a personal element into the text, showing the reader what they thought about design in general and how they applied their ideas to a variety of different gardens. They also show the degree to which garden design is often about people and relationships as much as plants or landscape. A successful partnership between designer and garden-owner has often been crucial to a garden's success, not least because the owner must uphold the designer's work long after he or she has departed.

The end result has been a century of rich industry and a series of outstanding gardens, all of which still survive and are likely to continue well into the future. It is hoped that the reader will be able to look at both the design principles discussed and the individual gardens, and take away both ideas and inspiration.

Part I
THE EVOLUTION OF CONTEMPORARY GARDEN DESIGN

(*Above*) Long Barn, Kent, Vita
Sackville-West's first garden.

(*Opposite*) Shrublands Hall, Suffolk,
where William Robinson altered
Charles Barry's classical designs.

The Start: Reaction to the Victorian Garden

It may seen unlikely that the contemporary garden evolved out of the Victorian era but fundamental roots were put down then which produced lasting growth. The abiding images from that time are gardens of display whose size and ingenuity concealed lack of originality in design. As in architecture the Victorians looked back for garden models and, for their country houses (both old and new), the Italian model was most favoured. At the same time engineering and industrial progress was applied to gardens with gusto: coal-fired boilers heated rows of glasshouses and ornate conservatories (the numbers of which soared after the abolition of the glass tax in 1845), and even the walls of kitchen gardens; steam-engines forced great jets of water out of fountains; and cast-iron, another Victorian breakthrough, became widely used for constructing garden buildings and furniture.

While they looked to the classical or medieval Gothic past for aesthetic models their taste also lent towards three essentials: the large scale, novelty, and

Ascott, Buckinghamshire, one of the Victorian homes of the Rothschilds, where bedding out of summer annuals was practised on a grand scale.

colour, all of which their gardens offered. Spectacular advances in propagation meant that plants could be raised in greenhouses for bedding out in summer, virtually unknown before the 1830s. By the 1860s skilful gardeners had progressed to the biannual system of a spring display followed by one in summer, as still practised today. And armies of gardeners – many worked solely in greenhouses propagating and tending – raised tens of thousands of plants which went out into intricate patterns of beds. The result could be brilliantly gaudy.

Another key advance of the period came in the transport of plants, originating with the Wardian case. Dr Nathaniel Bagshaw Ward discovered that plants in a sealed glass container transpired water which condensed and was then re-absorbed; a simple but crucial cycle which enabled plants to survive long journeys from overseas. The cases were in widespread use by the 1830s which meant the way was open for a flood of new plant introductions from overseas, satisfying the Victorian appetite for novelty. The most important came from temperate regions such as parts of the United States, New Zealand, China and the Himalayas, which adapted easily to British conditions and produced great families of hybrids. One has only to consider the rhododendrons – all of which have been successfully introduced – and coniferous trees of which Britain only has two native types, the Scots pine and English yew, to appreciate the scale of these introductions, the great majority of which began appearing around 1820.

The most exotic introductions were tender plants brought back from the more tropical regions of the world which would never survive the British climate. They presented gardeners with the challenge of first growing and then getting them to flower in artificially created surroundings. The most celebrated example was the Great Stove at Chatsworth in Derbyshire, which was designed and built between

Chatsworth's Great Stove, built by Joseph Paxton, was one of the gardening wonders of the Victorian age.

1836 and 1840 by the resident head gardener Joseph Paxton. At the time it was the largest area enclosed by glass in the world and became the prototype for Paxton's even more famous Crystal Palace.

The Great Stove was described by a visitor to Chatsworth in 1851:

'The conservatory at Chatsworth is filled with the rarest Exotics from all parts of the globe – from "farthest Ind", from China, from the Himalayas, from Mexico; here you see the rich banana, Eschol's grape, hanging in ripe profusion beneath the shadow of immense paper-like leaves, the feathery cocoa-palm, with its head peering almost to the lofty arched roof; the far-famed silk cotton-tree, supplying a sheet of cream-coloured blossoms, at a season when all outward vegetable gaiety is on the wane; the singular milk-tree of the Caraccas; the fragrant cinnamon and

cassia – with thousands of other rare and little known species of both flowers and fruit.'

In his last public duty before he died in 1861, Queen Victoria's husband Prince Albert opened the Royal Horticultural Society's Gardens in Kensington. The gardens were laid out to celebrate the society's elevation to royal status and they incorporated all the most fashionable designs of the period. They were strongly Italian in style with three different arcades surrounding three large descending terraces which contained formal water canals with ornate fountains, and a complicated series of designs with clipped box and yew topiary, and beds filled with coloured gravel to make patterns. Four depicted the national heraldic plants; the rose, thistle, leek and shamrock.

Initial admiration for the Kensington gardens soon turned to criticism and represented a growing tide of opinion looking for change, change that was to sow the seeds of the 20th-century garden. Before the late 1880s, when the Royal Horticultural Society allowed the site to be built on, it was clear that their show gardens were obsolete and had become the benchmark from which gardens must now progress. Critics argued that the ornate architectural features were lifeless copies, lacking quality of design or scale; that the beds of gravel and the over-fussy complexity of the patterns were artificial; and that horticultural interest was limited, more showpiece than garden.

Of course opulent gardens did not cease being created at once. A prime example was the splendid formal gardens laid out during the late 1870s in front of Baron Ferdinand de Rothschild's new château at Waddesdon in Buckinghamshire. The style was French rather than Italian but the overall

The relentless formality of the Royal Horticultural Society's gardens in Kensington (*top*) brought criticism to Victorian garden design. Nonetheless, lavish formality continued to be the style for many houses, such as Waddesdon Manor, Buckinghamshire, another Rothschild home (*bottom*).

composition was again made up of terraces with elaborate parterres decorated with fountain pools, urns and statues. One guest recalled staying there when a thunderstorm destroyed the bedding displays and the planting in the urns. By next morning the damaged plants had all been removed and replaced from the gardens' enormous greenhouses.

But incentive for change grew strongly, partly in terms of garden styles and, equally important, as a result of social pressure. By the 1870s the planting patterns that required annual bedding plants were extended with what is termed 'carpet-bedding'. Dwarf foliage plants – mainly new introductions from overseas raised in greenhouses – were planted in groups and clipped hard to give the effect of a patterned carpet. In fact the intricate patterns became more important than the historical accuracy of the design and many believed that the horticultural traditions of English gardens were being threatened.

Critics of the period Victorian garden had two strong arguments: the evidence of past history and the inspiration of gardens from nature. But they were comforted by the early 19th-century clear development towards informal, integrated gardens which Victorian displays had obscured but not eradicated. These developments, which had been suggested in the writing of two influential figures, Humphry Repton and John Claudius Loudon, now needed to be revived and encouraged. They complemented the other well-established tradition that gardens should in some way reflect nature. This did not mean a return to the ideals of the 18th-century landscape movement where nature had been idealized in expansive parkland schemes; it was more a recognition that the English countryside and the modest, traditional gardens it inspired were at least as relevant as the grandiose examples of past gardens in continental Europe.

The social impetus behind such sentiments was

clear at a number of levels. There was the widening of gardening interest which had gathered pace through the 19th century and the burgeoning middle classes of Victorian England representing an ever increasing number of people who wanted to have their own gardens. The exotic heights of fashion were not for them, and advice on how best to plan their own more modest domains and what they should contain gradually became increasingly available.

The title of Loudon's most widely read book, *The Surburban Gardener and Villa Companion* (1838), clearly confirms his readership. His wife Jane completed a notable partnership with her gardening books written specifically for women. *Gardening for Ladies* (1840) and its subsequent editions were equally popular in England and the United States. It was followed by *The Ladies' Companion to the Flower-Garden* (1841) and *The Ladies' Companion* periodical (begun in 1849) of which she was the first editor.

Loudon also founded the first popular gardening magazine, *Gardener's Magazine* (begun in 1826). After the flurry of periodicals that followed came the *Gardeners' Chronicle* (launched in 1841) with Joseph Paxton as its editor, which almost immediately achieved unrivalled supremacy. Paxton's designs for grandiose or expansive gardens and parks while writing for this new broad audience was an interesting illustration of Victorian social attitudes. He was not alone; in 1850 his assistant Edward Kemp published another book of wide-ranging influence, *How to Lay Out a Small Garden.*

Such popularizing of gardens was an important aspect of the changes wrought by England's increasingly industrialized, urban society. With more people living in oppressive, polluted towns so the desire to escape grew and the countryside became more and more attractive. Furthermore, the concept of the country garden increasingly became the ideal.

As social forces popularized gardens they also changed them at the upper levels. For centuries the gardens of the upper classes had been built on an unshakeable confidence in land and the security of a country estate. The agricultural depression that began in the 1880s, and which became the first of a constant succession, combined with growing democracy to undermine this confidence and bring about a clear reassessment. A different warning was posted by the number of Victorian industrialists who had built lavish country houses and gardens and consequently ruined themselves.

In the process of reassessment by no means everything was abandoned. The Victorian garden's most outspoken critic was William Robinson. He campaigned vociferously for the qualities of native English plants, for informal design and the cottage garden, not an Italian villa. But when commissioned in the 1880s to make alterations at Shrublands in

(Below) William Robinson's influence was more through his writing than his garden designs. At Shrublands *(opposite)* his alterations were to planting and did not affect Barry's architecture.

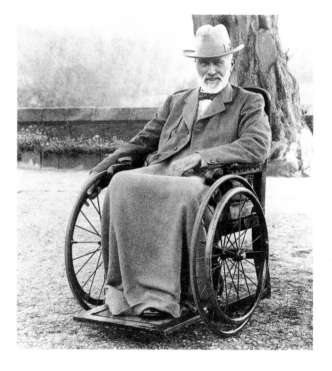

Suffolk, one of the most spectacular Victorian gardens (which had originally been laid out during the 1850s by Charles Barry, the doyen of Italianate-garden designers), Robinson worked within the existing architecture. He replaced the complex arrangement of bedding with lawn and more simplified borders. In his most successful book, *The English Flower Garden* (1883), Robinson even included a section on summer bedding.

Despite such lapses the Victorian garden underwent deep scrutiny and, in the period that followed, only what were seen as its good qualities were perpetuated. Garden designers continued to look to past periods for their models but they did so with an eye more sensitive to historical accuracy, balanced by originality and restraint in scale that were previously lacking. The widespread use of exotic plants was reduced but the Victorian example of grouping collections of rare trees in arboretums was built upon to produce gardens where far more varied collections of unusual plants were gathered. In simple terms the Victorian garden had demonstrated the limitless wealth of possibilities available to gardeners, but also the pitfalls of carrying these to excess. Avoiding these pitfalls became a guiding force for subsequent generations, and set the tone for future gardens.

Prior to Robinson, two of the most influential Victorian garden writers were John Loudon and his wife, Jane. His *Gardener's Magazine* pioneered popular garden journalism, while Jane's books were written to encourage women to garden.

From Arts and Crafts to the Edwardian Garden

William Robinson's opinions were loudly voiced in his books and the various periodicals he started or edited: *Garden* (which became part of *Homes and Gardens* in 1927); *Gardening Illustrated* (launched in 1879 and later merged with *Gardener's Chronicle*); *Cottage Gardening* (1848) and *Flora and Sylva* (1903). His ideas were therefore spread amongst a broad audience which was handed a new gardening outlook. Robinson's most lasting suggestion was his idea that a garden should combine in an uncontrived manner seasonal interest through the year with a degree of natural self-sufficiency and native, or at least hardy, plants. Two quotes illustrate his constantly repeated case. In one instance he suggested 'the placing of perfectly hardy exotic plants under conditions where they will thrive without further care' and in another he enthused about a cottage garden he had seen: 'no pretentious plan to consider, only the yellow sunflowers of the season massed in their own way.'

Criticism of garden design was part of a broader questioning of Victorian artistic taste. The umbrella for this reaction was the Arts and Crafts movement, born out of opposition to the factory system and advocating small-scale, hand-made craftsmanship. It looked back to Tudor and medieval times for its stylistic influence. Gardening was not seen as an industry but as an activity where mass-production should be stopped, as William Morris (one of the movement's leading figures) argued. 'Another thing too commonly seen is an aberration of the human mind, which otherwise I should have been afraid to warn you of. It is technically called carpet-gardening. Need I explain it further? I had rather not, for when I think of it even when I am quite alone I blush with shame . . .'

An important priority of the Arts and Crafts approach to gardens was a desire to end the standardization which became Victorian taste. The movement felt that gardens had been designed, planted and decorated to a formula, regardless of the house they surrounded, the site and the surrounding landscape. Herein lies a vital seed of the contemporary garden; the championing of variety in design and planting.

As a result numerous different threads of influence were incorporated, and the balance of formality and informality became more significant than reproducing any one particular period style. Gardens could hark back to Tudor and Stuart times, they could be more ambitious in scale and formal in layout, or they could use the cottage garden as an inspiration for old-fashioned planting and intimacy. But whichever path was chosen, the end result should be in harmony with house and setting.

Underlying the changes was the growing enthusiasm for the countryside. In 1890 J.D. Sedding wrote, 'everyone who can, now lives in the country, where he is bound to have a garden.' A year latter Sedding, an architect devoted to the ideals of the Arts and Crafts movement, published *Garden Craft Old and New* (1891), a book which embraced many of the ideas rising to prominence in gardening. As its title suggests, the book championed craftsmanship. It looked back romantically to old gardens, Elizabethan ones in particular: 'the old-fashioned garden represents one of the pleasures of England, one of the charms of that quiet beautiful life of bygone time that I, for one, would fain see revived.' Perhaps most importantly the book argued for unity between architecture and planting, and that one should not dominate the other.

An illustration from the book *Garden Craft Old and New* (1891) by J.D. Sedding, an Arts and Crafts devotee.

Comparable enthusiasms prompted the similar title of another book, *The Art and Craft of Garden Making* (1900). Its author was Thomas Mawson whose long career as a professional garden designer spanned the periods of the Arts and Crafts, the Edwardian garden, and the years between the wars, thereby providing important continuity. Mawson had started out as a humble nurseryman, was the first English professional garden designer to build up an international practice, and ended his career as the first President of the Institute of Landscape Architects in 1929, four years before his death. These developments, especially the international practice and the progression from designing private gardens to town planning and other larger landscape architecture schemes, pointed the way forward for many professional designers in the 20th century.

From around 1890 when his nursery practice,

Lakeland Nurseries at Windermere, spread into regular garden design work, Mawson was both prolific and successful. His huge number of commissions show that Edwardian England contained a large clientele able to spend impressive amounts of money on a new or rearranged garden. The scope of his activities was well illustrated in *The Art and Craft of Garden Making*. It provided detailed discussion of all aspects of garden design, illustrated with watercolours, photographs, plans and drawings.

The book was an impressive production and enjoyed instant success, running into five editions in a short period. Most of the places illustrated were the country houses of Mawson's affluent clients and some sections, for instance describing the treatment of entrance gates, lodges and driveways, have an immediately period style. But its outstanding feature was the breadth and detail of information on garden design: site surveying, different construction techniques for garden walls and their coping, endless possible designs for gates and gateways (both large and small), and long descriptive lists of trees and shrubs for gardens and parks, hardy climbing plants and hardy perennials, a wealth of information on all sizes of gardens. The book sales provided Mawson with the funds to open an office in London, besides his existing ones in Windermere and Lancaster, and thereafter country-house commissions appeared without break.

If there is any relevant generalization about Mawson's work it comes in his own description in *The Art and Craft of Garden Making* where he said he aimed for 'formality near the house, merging into the natural by degrees, so as to attach the house by imperceptible graduations to the general landscape.' In this Mawson saw himself maintaining continuity with Humphry Repton in the early 19th century, and he pinpointed what has become an enduring principle of garden design through the 20th century.

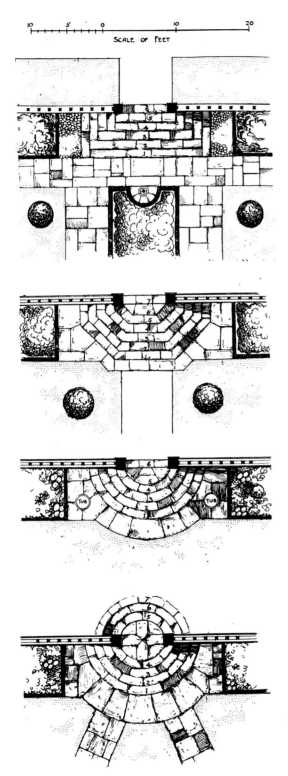

SCALE OF FEET

The Art and Craft of Garden Making (1900), by Thomas Mawson, was remarkable for its quantity of practical detail.

By allowing for limitless flexibility and adapting to the demands of different clients, Mawson also gained in popularity. Depending on their wishes they could have an architectural garden or water features, lawns for tennis and croquet, and any combination of rose gardens, borders, kitchen gardens and more naturally planted shrubberies or areas of woodland.

One constant factor through Mawson's work, which reflected his early Arts and Crafts training, was his emphasis on using local materials and vernacular building styles. A good example survives in his work at Wightwick Manor in Staffordshire in 1910, a half-timbered black and white house built in accurate Tudor style in 1887. Mawson extended the house's emphasis on timber to the garden by giving the retaining wall of the main terrace an unusual balustrade of oak. Depending on what part of the country he was working in, walls, where possible, were built of local stone or brick; garden buildings, gateways and other architectural features also reflected local building styles and that of the main house.

Mawson's work illustrated how the Arts and Crafts impetus, stimulated by opposition to what had gone before during the Victorian era, led fluently into the Edwardian period – when gardens became integral to the ethos of a country house or, more accurately, a house in the country lacking the former's size or status. Though enormously grand gardens were created during the period, they were usually built on the same principles that were applied to smaller ones.

Many gardens were strongly architectural before the First World War when building materials and labour were still easily affordable. It was not architecture for superficial display, however, but increasingly to provide a garden with a framework and to encourage a feeling of variety between one area and another. Walls were built to support terraces and, equally, to support climbing plants and provide the backdrop for a herbaceous border. The detail of brick or

stonework, semi-circular or square steps, was given as much attention as the combination of plants that were used in the border.

Thomas Mawson applied these principles of garden design with consummate professionalism, and possibly, as a result, his work has been criticized for lack of flair and originality. No such criticism is ever laid at the door of the partnership of Gertrude Jekyll and Edwin Lutyens, who met in 1889 and later followed similar principles but achieved more lasting and spectacular reputations. Their work took the inspiration of the Arts and Crafts movement and honed it into the foundation stone of the contemporary garden.

(*Opposite*) Wightwick Manor, where Mawson worked, was an important Arts and Crafts house and garden. (*Below*) Classical designs were equally popular at the time but without the quantity of Victorian decoration.

The partnership fused amateur and professional, horticulture and architecture.

In simple terms Jekyll was the amateur plantswoman, Lutyens the professional architect. But this explanation disguises the rich vein which their partnership opened up. Jekyll was brought up with an avant-garde interest in the arts and became a talented painter who developed a love of gardens at an early age. As an amateur who progressed from her own garden to advising others about theirs she set a standard of social acceptability for practical gardening by women. Her background and training as a painter gave her an early affinity with the Arts and Crafts movement. She was an admirer of William Robinson whom she knew well. Her work and writing perpetuated and developed his ideas, and for some years she edited his journal *The Garden*.

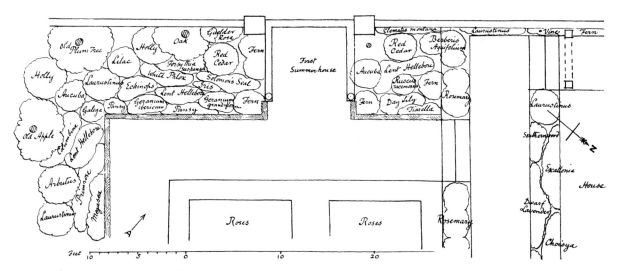

A detail of a Jekyll planting plan for Millmead, Surrey, showing her expert eye for plant associations.

(*Opposite*) Folly Farm, Berkshire, was one of Jekyll and Lutyens's most successful gardens.

In Jekyll's gardening and writing Robinson's crusading zeal soon disappeared and was replaced by a confident breadth of knowledge which set a rare standard. She applied the eye for colour developed in her painting to the arrangement of plants in a border and, better than anyone else, demonstrated how the small-scale intimacy of the cottage garden ideal could be adapted to, or developed for, any scheme. Equally important, garden design provided the scope for Jekyll to apply the knowledge and love of vernacular architecture and craftsmanship which she steadily developed.

The much younger Lutyens (he was 25 years her junior) was equally immersed in Arts and Crafts ideals through his training as an architect, but once his partnership with Jekyll got under way in the 1890s he demonstrated how his talents were ideally suited to the kind of house and garden harmony many increasingly desired. In his book *The Edwardian Garden* (1989) David Ottewill concluded: 'The Lutyens and Jekyll garden represents a synthesis of formal layout and natural planting unique in garden art. To his youthful genius for architectural form and geometric invention, she brought a mature understanding of the

crafts and an enthusiasm for vernacular and old-fashioned plants, which together produced a succession of enchanting designs, original in conception, perfect in scale and exquisite in colour and material.'

It is important to appreciate that the partnership's success was due not only to their respective talents but to timing. During the twenty-odd years from 1892 when Lutyens began designing Jekyll's house at Munstead Wood in Surrey – and they were most productive years – they had at their disposal a captive audience of potential clients. Given that most of the social and economic pre-requisites for their work disappeared with the First World War, the perpetuation of their ideas by enthusiastic successors is the most significant pointer to their lasting influence.

Lutyens's architectural talent was so precocious that he gained true satisfaction only when designing a house and garden as a composite whole; he constantly argued that one central idea should dictate the style of both and their points of unity. His attention to detail became so obsessive that he would even agonize for ages over the design for the handle of a wooden garden gate. But his overriding contribution was sheer originality of design and although often

fiercely architectural, the best gardens Lutyens created with Jekyll did not depend on size for their success. On the contrary they were surprisingly small and it was the balanced scale which allowed for the integration of a sometimes bewildering quantity of different areas and features.

Scale, and the softening effect of Jekyll's planting schemes, were planned in minute detail. Her spidery designs, which included the names of plants in their allotted places, represented her growing accumulation of plant knowledge through experiment and observation. Many 20th-century gardeners describe their plants as personalities and Jekyll was probably the first to do so. She wrote about them in such a way, describing their individual characteristics, suggesting how they could be grouped with others, commenting on suitable positions and soils, as to educate her readers into a quite new approach to gardening. Jekyll's priority was always to look at a site and decide what to plant, not to take a certain plant and wonder where to put it.

Whereas Victorian gardeners might plant out annual bedding flowers in rows of adjacent monochrome to reproduce the same colour endlessly, Jekyll demonstrated with hardy plants that one colour was best appreciated in association with other shades. She also showed that where planting one particular variety or shade, the choice of foliage – its shape and shade of green – was of paramount importance, being the only contrast to the flower colour. Such apparently simple maxims have become cornerstones of the contemporary garden, with successful plant association more highly valued than any one plant's individual qualities.

Jekyll and Lutyens often demonstrated that they were well able to design along classical lines. She had

Sir George Sitwell looked directly to Italy for inspiration for the classical garden he created at Renishaw, Derbyshire.

made drawing expeditions to Italy and knew and admired that country's gardens. Their most notable classical collaboration was probably Hestercombe in Somerset, but from around 1910 Lutyens increasingly moved towards strong classicism in his architecture. During his later career, by which time Jekyll had retired into peaceful isolation at Munstead Wood, the style of his houses and gardens was often monumentally classical, lacking the warm intimacy that had once made their joint designs so appealing.

The Edwardian period witnessed an enthusiasm for Italian gardens in both England and the United States, but with fundamental differences from those Italianate gardens created by Victorians such as Charles Barry. The Edwardian gardeners admired Italian gardens for their architectural qualities and in the way they evoked the landscape. Rather than reproduce them derivatively they adapted specific Italian styles and features to an English setting, creating gardens that were both historical and original. In doing so they ensured that the Italian inspiration was able to throw off its dull Victorian image and survive into the 20th century.

This rejuvenation of the Italian ideal was achieved most effectively by Harold Peto who in 1892 gave up his fashionable architect's practice to concentrate on interior and, in particular, garden design. Peto's childhood home had been Somerleyton Hall in Suffolk which his railway magnate father, Sir Samuel, adorned with legendary Victorian gardens. His son's gardening affections were more fastidious and he strongly objected to the gardening styles of his father's generation. Writing of his favoured Italian style he concluded that 'If more of our English gardens could have an increase of this influence it would be well, instead of their running riot in masses of colour irrespective of form.'

As with Lutyens and Thomas Mawson, many of Peto's architectural features such as loggias, elegant

pavilions and summerhouses were period pieces; affordable to Edwardians but prohibitively expensive for subsequent generations of gardeners. But his contribution to garden design proved lasting in two particular areas: the incorporation of architectural formality into a landscape setting without the latter losing its natural qualities, and the idea that a garden could be a repository for architectural curiosities. Many 20th-century gardens, especially small town ones, incorporate a single ornamental feature like an urn, a sundial or well-head to give a point of emphasis or a contrast to the planting. In his own Wiltshire garden at Iford Manor created from the turn of the century Peto arranged his large collection of architectural items around the garden's terraces, skilfully juxtaposing them with carefully chosen planting.

H. Avray Tipping, a garden designer and writer whose articles in *Country Life* and column in the *Morning Post* made him one of the most influential garden writers of the Edwardian period, believed 'if the relative spheres and successful inter-marriage of formal and natural gardening are better understood today than ever before, that desirable result is due to the efforts of no one man more than to Mr Peto'. As exemplified by Peto and the best of his contemporaries – Lutyens, Jekyll and Mawson – it was one of the prime garden design legacies of the Edwardian period. The other, which they all similarly advocated, was the maximum harmony between house and garden; whether the two were linked by architecture or planting could be left to individual taste.

Harold Peto's garden designs gave country houses such as Heale in Wiltshire, illustrated here, an elegant setting that was Italian in style yet suited to the English countryside.

Classicism and Modernism

From the late 19th century many Americans had been keen admirers of Italian gardens. Two of their number wrote the two major books on the subject at the turn of the century: Charles Platt's *Italian Gardens* (1894) and Edith Wharton's *Italian Villas and their Gardens* (1903). This admiration combined with a general enthusiasm for European culture to produce a strongly classical style of garden design well suited to the demands of wealthy American clients; their new houses and gardens were status symbols in the way they had been for English Victorians. Through

The grotto garden at Villa Gamberaia, from Edith Wharton's influential book *Italian Villas and their Gardens* (1903).

the decades leading up to the First World War this classical style of garden design was demonstrated in the Beaux-Arts tradition that took its name from the Paris school which reached the peak of its reputation during the late 19th century.

Beaux-Arts garden design was distinctive in two ways. It subjected natural landscape to architectural symmetry in a manner deemed suitable for the surroundings to buildings, and its classicism was strongly decorative. The gardens were conceived as architectural wholes, axially linked, with a uniformity of style and repetition of decorative features such as balustraded terraces, classical statues and Corinthian or other classical effects. The French had demonstrated how the style could be enlarged for the design of public parks with the layout of the Bois de Boulogne and other similar Parisian gardens, and their example was enthusiastically taken up in the United States in both public gardens and those surrounding château-style country houses.

The overall effect was imposing, often spectacularly so, and ideally suited to plutocratic taste. But with the onset of the Great Depression in 1929 the economic wherewithal and social confidence for such lavish displays vanished and garden design underwent a reappraisal that had long-term effects. The slump took hold as modern architecture was becoming established and many American garden designers, who were to become the most influential figures of their generation, progressed from the classicism of their Beaux-Arts training to modernism.

They were able to do so more readily and adventurously than their European contemporaries who were encumbered by entrenched gardening traditions

Built over a waterfall, the Kauffmann house, in Fallingwater, Pennsylvania, sought to merge architecture with the landscape.

that stretched back for centuries. Inspired by the architecture of Le Corbusier, and more especially the American Frank Lloyd Wright, they applied the same emphasis on spatial arrangement and abstract or organic shapes to garden design. In contrast to the imposed nature of Beaux-Arts classicism the relationship between a garden and the surrounding landscape assumed paramount importance. For American designers the landscape was not the picturesque countryside of England but often something far more expansive and untamed.

At the same time the domestic, functional nature of private gardens was acknowledged as never before.

The Edwardian garden had accommodated such social recreations as tennis, croquet and swimming. Now – especially in areas with warm climates like California – the garden was actually planned as an outdoor extension of the house, an extra room or series of rooms where planting was fitted into a practical design.

The new direction that these designers were seeking aimed to change what one of their number, Fletcher Steele, targeted when he wrote, 'the chief vice in gardens is merely to be pretty.' Steele was steeped in Beaux-Arts training at the Harvard School of Landscape Architecture and extended his knowledge by visiting European gardens. During the 1920s he remained faithful to his background designing the classical gardens that were still fashionable. One of his first major designs was a garden with a long bowling green walk from the house to a large circular pool, enclosed by a balustrade, with a spectacular fountain jet. One visitor to the garden remarked enthusiastically that, of all the gardens in the United States, it was 'the only place that she knew of that had the charm of the age-old gardens of Europe'.

Steele's admiration for European gardens did not disappear, as is evident in his design for the garden of Charlotte Witney Allen in Rochester, New York, which he worked on from the 1920s to '50s, and which was clearly inspired by Italian Renaissance gardens like the Villa Marlia. But he progressed to a less predictable and ornate style, which also acknowledged the influences of gardens outside Europe. He was an avid traveller who visited Europe annually for many years and also made trips to Japan and China, whose gardens subsequently influenced his work.

Steele described the new modern architectural influences that affected his garden design in the following terms: 'I care much for the shape, size and proportion of the empty air spaces of my gardens and guard them jealously. Otherwise I am ready to let the

client choose the enframing "style". Planting is chosen to bring out and enhance the size, proportions and colour of the spaces.'

Thomas Church underwent a similar Beaux-Arts training as Steele, also at Harvard, but made an even more decisive break when he set up his own practice in San Francisco in 1930. Church established the 'California School' of garden design and acquired an enormous reputation on the small private gardens of San Francisco. They remained his primary area of interest through his career which lasted until within a few years of his death in 1978.

In Church's work the most contemporary concerns and limitations for designers and garden owners alike were confronted and overcome in an entirely original style. The confines of a small urban space, desire for privacy, the requirements of children and need for low maintenance were all meticulously addressed. Church's philosophy was encapsulated in the title of

Fletcher Steele's Beaux-Arts training was evident in his designs for the Charlotte Whitney Allen garden, both in a preliminary sketch for a tent pavilion (*above left*) and in the finished garden (*above*). Thomas Church's neat, balanced small gardens (*opposite*) give a picture of uncluttered elegance.

his first and most important book, *Gardens are for People* (1955). It illustrates one garden in particular which Church designed around a circular track for a child's tricycle. Church had worked out that 'One thing is certain: a circular route in the garden can provide more amusement hours for small children than any number of swings or slides.' Other gardens and their features were planned around other contemporary priorities with similar practicality. Of the transition from house to garden via steps he once remarked, 'It should be safe enough so you don't wish you'd worn your duck-hunting boots, and safe enough so you don't spill your lemonade.'

Limited area led Church to experiment with exaggerated angular shapes, such as a bold L-shaped path dividing lawn and border, which effectively gave the illusion of greater space. Another means of achieving this was to leave the main central area – which was usually asymmetrical in shape – as simple gravel, paving, or wooden decking suitable to the Californian surroundings. The Californian climate also encouraged his minimal use of grass and his liking for other materials such as redwood decking. The functional simplicity of these gardens, especially those where gravel was the central medium, was strongly reminiscent of Japanese Zen gardens. Even within the smallest garden Church's skill with plants enabled him to maximize their effect. They were selected as much for their shape and appearance through the year as for any particular flower quality.

Thomas Church's garden design was inspired by the landscape and climate of California where he worked almost exclusively, and encouraged him to break away from the long-established classical traditions of European gardens which had developed in the United States. But for designer Beatrix Farrand these traditions were to be built upon within the demands of an individual site, and her work in the United States and England provides an important link between the Edwardian garden and the late 20th century.

Farrand was a niece of the American novelist Edith Wharton. Formal training at the Arnold Arboretum in the 1880s followed a background influenced by regular visits to Europe. The most formative was in 1895 when she visited Gertrude Jekyll at Munstead Wood, and Jekyll's influence on her choice and arrangement of plants is evident through her career. As well as her own gardens her most important contribution to the history of garden design came when she purchased the majority of Jekyll's plans and drawings which she passed on to the University of California at Berkeley, shortly before she died in 1959.

This safeguarding of such a vital gardening heirloom exemplified the manner in which Farrand's career provided a bridge between European and American gardens, and adapted the legacy of Jekyll to the inter-war period and later. Just as Jekyll was a pioneering figure in England, establishing a role for the amateur woman gardener as garden designer or garden writer, so too was Beatrix Farrand in the United States. In 1899 when still in her twenties she was the only woman among the twelve founder members of the American Society of Landscape Architects. But garden design and planting rather than large-scale landscape architecture were always Farrand's primary interest and their importance is immediately evident in her designs of the public gardens at the universities of Princeton, Yale, and Harvard, all of which she worked on intermittently from the early 1900s.

In her private garden designs Farrand often worked around old houses within an existing garden landscape. She demonstrated a sensitivity to a place's history and establishment, balanced with a keen eye for

how change could be beneficial, in a manner that set standards for future 20th-century garden designers who would be regularly confronted with similar projects.

In her American gardens the most important achievement was the move forward from copying European styles to integrating their traditions – from classical Italy or France, or English Arts and Crafts – into designs which, especially in their choice of plants and harmony with the surrounding landscape, were strongly indigenous. And while she constantly acknowledged her debt to Jekyll, Farrand's gardens were markedly less architectural than those of the Jekyll–Lutyens partnership, illustrating how both in England and America the tendency was increasingly towards an understated garden structure.

In England another American, Lawrence Johnston, was creating a garden where the use of hedges to provide a living, changing structure rather than an inanimate architectural one was raised to new heights. Johnston, who became a naturalized Englishman in 1900, began his garden at Hidcote in Gloucestershire shortly after purchasing the property in 1907. But the garden's style and character belong to the period after the First World War when it was continued and completed; there is no hint of the leisured abundance of an Edwardian garden.

Johnston was a self-taught owner-gardener helped at Hidcote by Norah Lindsay, a flamboyant aristocrat who continued the tradition of English amateur-professional gardeners begun by Gertrude Jekyll. Together Johnston and Lindsay built upon Jekyll's example, developing new styles of planting and emphasizing the division of a garden into enclosures, each with its own character and appearance. The

At Hidcote, Gloucestershire, Lawrence Johnston's blend of intimate scale, formality of design and variety of planting illustrated a style of gardening that could be adapted to any size and became a landmark for the 20th-century garden.

balance between firm design and rich planting which had been encouraged by the Arts and Crafts movement and put into practice by many Edwardian designers was developed in a way that future English gardeners constantly followed.

Johnston was rich enough to design his garden to the highest standards and go on expeditions abroad – often accompanied by his cook, chauffeur and valet – to collect rare plants. But he wanted to make the garden himself, not hire others to do everything. In the early stages he drove the tractor to grade the farmland into suitable terrain and later planted a large proportion of the many thousands of plants. Such active involvement became an increasing trend through the 20th century with the result that many gardens increasingly gained a personal style and character. Towards the end of Johnston's life Hidcote also became a major landmark in the appreciation of gardens; in 1948 it became the first to be accepted by the National Trust purely on its own merits, not because it was a country-house package.

The cult of personality gardens reached a climax with Vita Sackville-West's Sissinghurst creation in

(*Left*) Vita Sackville-West with her two sons, Nigel (on the left) and Ben, at Long Barn, Kent. Close to her childhood home of Knole, Long Barn (*above*) was her gardening apprenticeship before Sissinghurst.

became reality with the survival of both creators well into the post-war period.

Writing about the inevitable tendency to link Hidcote and Sissinghurst, Jane Brown accurately commented that 'people love Sissinghurst, but they admire Hidcote' The affection for Sissinghurst is as human as it is horticultural. The background of Vita's childhood at the historic family home of Knole, her instilled love of the Kent countryside and her poetry made it only natural that she should purchase the derelict remnants of a Tudor castle (in 1930) and transform its wilderness into a paradise garden. The husband and wife partnership, the neat, sober designs by Harold and the ebullient planting by Vita, further enrich the cocktail.

As the Arts and Crafts movement looked back nostalgically to periods before the onset of Victorian excess, so Sissinghurst perpetuated this mood and ensured that the cult of the romantic would remain integral to 20th-century English garden design. Vita wrote her literary masterpiece, the epic poem *The Garden*, during the Second World War, an experience which prompted her to regard her garden as a personal haven. This idea of escape from the ugly outside world has burgeoned through the post-war decades and influenced many people's approach to garden design.

Many of the tangible features of garden design progressed naturally from the Arts and Crafts and Edwardian periods to those that followed. But there was a discernible shift in people's expectations: previously a garden's appearance and style were sufficient to provide enjoyment; for later generations a certain mood has been increasingly sought. The variety in design styles that this encouraged clearly began between the wars. The sense of a garden as a personal haven of tranquillity, planted to individual taste, is as evident in a small town garden in San Francisco by Thomas Church as it is at Sissinghurst.

Kent. Indeed this aspect of the garden has contributed hugely to its enduring, legendary reputation. But the lionizing is a relatively recent development and the garden was originally known only to the friends of Vita and her husband Harold Nicolson, and the gardening cognoscenti. The story of Sissinghurst's creation and its potent romanticism was destined to break radically new ground in people's attitudes to creating a garden, a likelihood that

The Post-War Garden: Quality in Variety

The post-war decades have confirmed another development that had begun before the Second World War, that private gardens would provide only one area of activity for garden designers. As munificent private-garden owners willing or able to commission ambitious schemes became increasingly rare, public projects – gardens for new towns, for offices and parks – arose to provide the new profession of landscape architect with an alternative brief. Partly inspired by a desire to offer a human but functional response to landscape demands, rather than one provided by a mix of garden architecture and planting, landscape architecture seemed to hint at a conflict between new ideas and established garden traditions.

In the event, instead of conflict there has been a steady widening of the gardening spectrum and it has become acknowledged that different answers are suitable for different situations; it is unrealistic to design a garden for a country rectory or manor house with the same recipe as for a tiny town garden or an urban public space.

All this is illustrated by the career of Sylvia Crowe which began with private garden design during the 1930s and expanded to monumental landscaping projects, such as siting reservoirs and electricity power-lines. In her book *Garden Design* (1958) she argued that the garden was where men expressed their feelings for their surroundings and landscape; she referred to private gardens as 'the gloriettas of individual man'. At the same time the book's successive chapters make it clear that whatever intangible qualities gardeners should strive for, on a practical level the sources of inspiration for the contemporary gardener had become limitless.

In terms of the evolution of garden design the steady broadening of ideas has meant that they lead less and less in any one particular direction. Gardens have been increasingly designed and planted to individual taste and the limitations of a site, few people having either the means or confidence to make dramatic changes to the land. More often than not the source of inspiration has been a specific garden not an aesthetic or historical idea, thus contributing enormously to reputations of the select few such as Hidcote and Sissinghurst which very quickly became role models.

The idea that the curving lines of an enclosed city garden continue the 18th-century tradition of

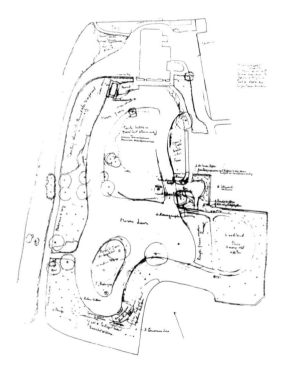

Brenda Colvin's design for a garden in Combe, Berkshire, combined mown and longer grass containing spring bulbs.

'Capability' Brown's sinuous lakes and tree plantations is not always easily appreciated. But seeing a group of trees and shrubs in a meadow setting, or one of Vita Sackville-West's combinations of climbers on a brick wall at Sissinghurst, is a tangible inspiration.

As a result a garden's quality, or lack of it, depends not on any one style which has entered the free market, but on the application of certain accepted principles of design. In the lofty tone which characterizes *Garden Design* Sylvia Crowe emphasized this when she wrote that 'underlying all the greatest gardens are certain principles of composition which remain unchanged because they are rooted in the natural laws of the universe'. In a more immediate sense the principles which had been honed in successive hands through the 20th century involved scale, and plant association and harmony between the formal and informal, often through the juxtaposition of architecture and planting.

And yet, as if to redress the balance and pre-empt criticism, the contemporary approach to gardens has been strongly influenced by moral landscape dilemmas, arriving out of the connection between professional landscape architecture and garden design. Crowe's contemporary and fellow pioneer of fully-fledged professionalism for women designers, Brenda Colvin, highlighted this in her book *Land and Landscape* (1948) in which she gave early voice to environmental concerns now universally accepted: 'The control that man is able to exert over his environment is so great that we easily overlook the power of the environment over man . . . We know that man can ruin his surroundings and make them unsuitable for future generations, but we continue to act as if we did not know it, and we have not properly mastered the methods which the elementary knowledge should lead us to apply.'

Much of Colvin's work as a landscape architect confronted her with such awkward environmental dilemmas and in reaction her garden design excelled in gentle plant associations. Her chosen favourites were usually simple perennial varieties, many either still to be found growing wild in the countryside or old-fashioned traditional plants that had metaphorically hopped out of the meadow into the cottage garden. Colvin was gardening in this way during the 1950s and was an early champion of informal wildflower planting that has become popular in recent years. As Vita Sackville-West found refuge from the war at Sissinghurst so Colvin encouraged the idea of the garden as a haven where threatened nature could be secure in miniature.

These concerns have been shared by another contemporary of Crowe and Colvin, Geoffrey Jellicoe, and similarly, if differently, influenced his garden design. Jellicoe's career encapsulates all the diversity and dilemmas that have grown up around contemporary garden design. Trained as an architect he formed an early, abiding admiration for Italian Renaissance

At Shute House Geoffrey Jellicoe formalized one stretch of the stream into a canal ending in arched grottoes with classical statues.

gardens through detailed study and his work continuously upholds the traditions of classicism. At the same time he developed an equal affinity with abstract modern art which he has expressed in his designs wherever possible. Jellicoe's prime motivation, however, has been provided by man's relation to the natural landscape, a Herculean subject which he addressed most particularly in his book *The Landscape of Man* (1975).

Jellicoe has explored this fragile relationship in all his work as a landscape architect and, in microcosm, in his garden design. By his own admission he has never been a plantsman and in all his designs the planting has been the work of another, often his wife Susan. The essence of Jellicoe's work is his vision of gardens and landscape as an evolutionary process in which man has always been intrinsically involved, imposing himself in varying ways at different times.

With this philosophy Jellicoe has been as comfortable with great classical garden schemes for which his architectural training prepared him, as with the abstract shapes of modernism. Perhaps most important, his designs have striven to demonstrate that the earliest human gardens were created as much for symbolic reasons as to provide visible beauty and pleasure, and that this symbolism has evolved cyclically into the contemporary garden.

Early in his career Jellicoe worked in partnership with Russell Page, and the divergence of their paths well illustrates the broad spectrum of post-war garden design. Page was drawn into garden design by an early love of plants. He trained briefly as an artist in Paris which prompted his return to France after the war where he established a one-man design practice until 1962. In many ways Page's work perpetuated the fastidious connoisseurship of

Longleat, Wiltshire, was one of Russell Page's early garden designs. The elegant lines of pleached limes and yew hedges became hallmarks of his work.

Lawrence Johnston's Hidcote, and the precise formalism of French gardens which strongly influenced his work combined with his horticulture to produce work notably restrained.

Indeed restraint was Page's watchword as he repeatedly made clear through the chapters of his elegant, classic gardening book, *The Education of a Gardener* (1962). It is significant that the book's first chapter opens with a sentence reiterating the belief of Jellicoe and so many of their contemporaries: 'Garden-making, like gardening itself, concerns the relationship of the human being to his natural surroundings.' He knew what were the pitfalls: 'We live under the accumulation of periods and styles and cultures . . . a vast store of information making a vast confusion.' And he was equally certain of the best approach: 'All the good gardens I have ever seen, all the garden scenes that have left me satisfied were the result of just such reticence; a simple idea developed as far as it could be.'

Page's fastidious approach to his work set important standards at a time when much English garden design was descending into confusion: curving lines and uneven shapes, and uncomfortable mixing of all types of plants – shrubs, perennials, annuals and bulbs – to produce a picture of restless untidiness rather than the hoped-for richness. Once again he located the problem: 'Another reason for the frequent lack of consideration given to the underlying structure of contemporary gardens is that modern gardeners have a far greater choice of plants. The élite among them know and care for rare and unusual plants which they have collected and cultivated with care and skill. However, they tend to be less interested in the visual relationships of form and colour.' The last comment echoes sentiments expressed by Gertrude Jekyll more than half a century earlier.

Page's response was to approach the plants he used considering their shape and form in equal proportion to their colour. The use of plants, either singly or in hedges, to give architectural structure to a garden – which Johnston did to such brilliant effect at Hidcote – fitted perfectly into Page's idea of good design, while the flowering plants he used were meticulously chosen and often used in single colours.

His favourite combination was a blend of formal planting, with architectural terraces and steps, and symmetrical water features which inevitably produced an immaculate overall impression. He also demonstrated in many gardens how the clean-cut lines of his designs, borders contained within low box hedging parallel to a paved path, could accommodate more abstract, modernist shapes.

The international nature of Page's career meant that his commissions came from an ever-increasing web of connections; the success of one new garden led to requests for others. This also facilitated the interchange of different styles of garden from one country to another which has become part of the variety of contemporary garden design. Page designed quintessentially English herbaceous borders for country gardens in France and geometric French *jardins potager* for English manors.

An easy succession of clients, as one country house commission led to another, was also the happy lot of Lanning Roper, who probably worked in more English country gardens than any other post-war designer. This is the more remarkable when one remembers that he was an American who first came to England when serving in the American navy during the Second World War. Roper developed an unerring feel for what has developed into a major thread of post-war design; creating from new, rejuvenating, or restoring all or part of a garden around an old-established country home. Roper's gardens

A border planted by Lanning Roper at Chartwell, Kent, shows how effectively he mixed herbaceous plants and flowering shrubs in large, low-maintenance borders.

perpetuated the border planting of Gertrude Jekyll and Norah Lindsay, but subtly adapted them to accommodate a more contemporary approach to plant association and colour choice.

The mixed border, with large shrubs surrounded by boldly grouped perennials and grey foliage plants spilling out in front across a path or lawn edge, became something of a calling-card as most of his best designs still testify. The reasoning behind their construction was not only visual pleasure; once the borders had filled out to maturity they often required minimum maintenance and Roper's work provided important evidence that lack of resources – human or mechanical – need not mean lower visual standards.

Roper, like Thomas Mawson at the beginning of the century, was always prepared to put a client's requirements first and design to a given brief. While this did much to account for his popularity, accompanying advice on how to make the best of any given design was at the heart of his success. At a garden in Yorkshire he advised the owners who had pulled down an unmanageably large Victorian house and replaced it with a smaller neo-Georgian one. They wished to retain tangible reminders of the old house and so Roger planned the garden with new borders along partly rebuilt walls which marked the outlines of the old house, and retained the six-pillared portico in its original position as a folly.

The success of Roper's career right up until his death in 1983 illustrated that the garden ideal of a place in the country remained as powerful an attraction and motivation as it had been for advocates of

A group of narcissus, hellebores and euphorbias growing out of gravel at Denmans, Sussex.

the Arts and Crafts movement, and devotees of Edwardian country house life. This is confirmed in the work of John Brookes, which at the same time demonstrates the broadening of the spectrum of post-war garden design. Whereas Roper's work in simplified terms can be seen as the English manor with lawns and borders, Brookes has worked less on the surroundings of traditional country houses and his approach has clear similarities with Thomas Church's view of the garden as an extension of the house, which is confirmed by the title of his first book, *Room Outside* (1969).

In Brookes's gardens the terrace – traditionally constructed as a launching point from house to garden – becomes both intimate and enticing, an ebullient mixture of planted containers, climbers and garden furniture. The sense of progression from house to garden is encouraged by a change in the terrace's surface material and a path continuing the paving into the garden, and by a brick arch or small pergola which recalls the loggias so favoured by Lutyens.

Brookes trained under both Brenda Colvin and Sylvia Crowe in the 1950s and his approach to garden design combines the views of the landscape architect with those of the plantsman. The variety of his commissions is important because it demonstrates that in the post-war period a greater range of situations have suggested a particular type of response than ever was the case before. Indeed, one of the overriding messages of Brookes's many highly influential books is the importance of choosing a garden design that suits both landscape and house besides being practical.

A number of Brookes's designs have been adventurously modern; in the 1960s his courtyard garden for the new Penguin Books building in Middlesex was hailed as a rare example of modern art being applied to landscape. The design had been prompted by a geometric abstract drawing by Piet Mondrian whose shapes Brookes transposed into different mediums of

his design: planting, paving, grass and water. The garden has stood the test of time because of the quality of materials used, and because the treatment of the courtyard site entirely suited the setting.

The most enduring test of garden design during the post-war decades, as opposed to earlier periods, has been the small size of an increasing number of gardens whose owners are seeking a satisfying, perhaps innovative plan. Brookes is one of many designers who have followed Thomas Church's example and demonstrated that in the small garden quality and clarity of both design and planting are paramount. The Danish-born designer Preben Jakobsen has also made significant contributions to this area from the 1960s and in the process has highlighted an unlikely combination of historical and modern inspiration in the two figures of Lutyens and the Finnish architect and designer, Alvar Aalto. Unlikely because Aalto was one of the foremost modernist architects while Lutyens's work was rooted in the traditions of English vernacular, but they are comparable because of their similar feel for different materials and ingenious combinations.

This has been a strong feature of Jakobsen's work and has enhanced his style of designing a small area around a single architectural shape, which is repeated in different sizes and materials to give emphasis and depth to the picture. The angular shape of closely patterned paths or brick-edged beds is balanced by planting schemes chosen for foliage and striking individual shape a form, the limited space not often allowing for extensive plant association in one area. Jakobsen demonstrated that the practical requirement for the majority of unplanted areas in a small garden involves hard materials rather than more traditional but less resilient grass, and can provide the opportunity for innovation and thereby heighten the garden's atmosphere and appearance.

Besides Jakobsen's handling of architectural hard

materials on a small scale, his emphasis on plants, however limited their number, illustrates the note of continuity that has flowed through the contemporary garden from the Arts and Crafts movement. Throughout the successive periods the choice of plants, their grouping, their use with architectural features and even water has been the yardstick of good design. Few would create even the most functional small modern garden without a plant presence to provide life and seasonal change; originality is always possible because no planting scheme can be precisely reproduced.

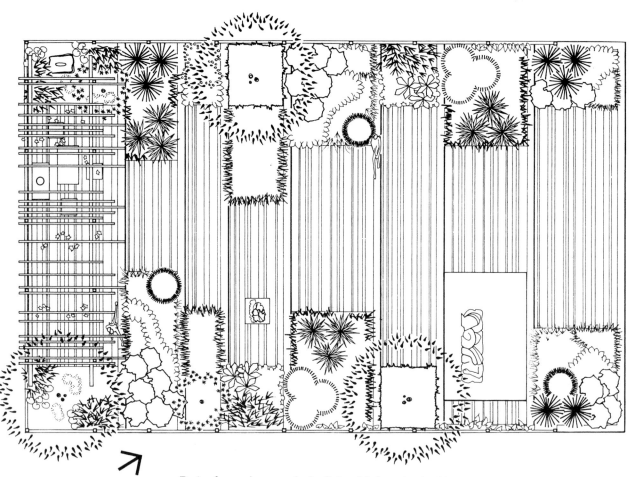

Design for a sculpture garden by Preben Jakobsen showing his combinations of geometric and abstract shapes on a small scale.

The Future:
Garden and Landscape as One

The partnership of Wolfgang Oehme and James van Sweden, launched in 1977, has been credited with founding a 'New American Garden' style which aims to continue the evolution of garden design in a vigorous fashion. Both partners have training and experience in Europe and the United States, but their aspirations are largely founded in a desire to progress from the current mainstream of American gardens. One commentator has described the move as being 'away from the aristocratic European model towards a reflection of the egalitarian United States and its great plains heritage'.

Wolfgang Oehme was born in Germany where he trained and worked before emigrating to Baltimore and joining a landscape architecture practice. James van Sweden was born and trained in the United States, but he also extended his experience to Europe with work in the Netherlands. This cross-matching of American and European garden developments with private garden design and urban landscape work (public parks and urban regeneration) became vital influences on their future designs.

An important realization was that urban landscape architecture benefitted from a high gardening input, a concentration on the use of plants and not just creating a satisfactory open space. This resulted in approaching both public and private garden design with the same objective. Public gardens should fulfil the same requirements for the casual passer-by as a small private garden would for its owner. The success of this approach depended on individual features and areas being planned on a human scale. In this way, however large the overall scheme, its component parts would be immediately accessible in the manner of a private garden. In their own words, 'Nature's unfolding drama belongs to all people, especially those without access to home gardening . . . They like to feel surrounded by a loose screen of plants, protected and not endangered. Whether public or private, the principles of spatial layering and temporal change are what makes a garden a garden. These principles create a human scale that mediates between nature and the city.'

The primary step forward in Oehme and van Sweden's work is their rejection of accepted styles of grouping and displaying plants in formal borders or flower-beds, and in association with architectural features, clipped trees and hedges. Instead they advocate that the primary inspiration for both gardens and larger landscape designs lies in the natural landscape: the choice, arrangement and treatment of plants and their association with water and hard architectural features should be guided by this overriding priority. Their gardens aim to create the illusion of natural American meadow with large single blocks of perennial plants grouped together, allowed to develop through their natural annual cycle without training, pruning or shaping.

In many ways their work draws together a number of themes that have evolved through the 20th century. The prairie style developed between the wars in the mid-west landscapes of Jens Jensen, who planted parks and large gardens with native hardwood trees, is the height of simple naturalism, depending for its effect on the seasonal change in foliage and branch shape. Oehme and van Sweden feel this has been stifled by the continuous demand for traditional decorative styles of garden. Thomas Church's championing

of the garden as a place that combines human activity with horticulture in a manner best suited to each site (however small) and each client, unaffected by current fashion, has been similarly important. Fusing these two original and important extremes of American garden style has been a major achievement of Oehme and van Sweden's work.

Although motivated by a desire to influence American gardens, their ideas are applicable elsewhere, and the environmental landscape concerns that they address are contemporary rather than national. They deliberately avoid manicuring in any sense whether it be a large area of carefully mown lawn, clipped yew hedges or topiary, or carefully staked/tied border plants or even climbers. Their planting schemes are chosen to be, if necessary, naturally self-sufficient through an annual season and – highly relevant today – they require no use of pesticides or herbicides. The selection of plants and emphasis on initial soil preparation ensure that plants are immediately well-established and able to develop into the energetic communities of shapes and textures which Oehme and van Sweden always encourage.

They write characteristically of their planting ideas in their book *Bold Romantic Gardens* (1990): 'Low-growing perennials are most numerous, creating a lush and undulating "ground-cover". Pendulous grasses like *Pennisetum alopecuroïdes* may overlap and soften pools, walls and walks. Taller special (including grasses, perennials and shrubs) create a partial enclosure, while trees signal transitions and boundaries, and frame the house within the garden. Not only are you surrounded in every direction with an ever-changing panorama, but the plantings are composed so that you can see them from every side.

An Oehme and van Sweden design which demonstrates how they create unity between architecture, garden and surrounding landscape using a combination of simple geometric lines, ornamental features and striking plant shapes.

Masses of plants undulate from low to high as they move from front to back to side to side, leading the eye through the composition.'

Part of the evolution of the contemporary garden has been a process of distilling influences into suitable ideas and designs. In this sense Oehme and van Sweden have built on the growing admiration for Japanese gardens to incorporate their contemplative simplicity, the maximizing of a single feature to make an important statement as a recurring theme in their garden design. It is perhaps no surprise that the species of one of Oehme and van Sweden's favourite plants, the perennial grass *Miscanthus sinensis*, grows wild on lowland Japanese hillsides. The horticultural riches of Japan combine with their gardening ethos which gives a meaning to each individual element and the simplest or smallest of combinations. Comparing Japan with the United States, Oehme and van Sweden write: 'Because Japanese culture is highly tuned to ephemera . . . their gardens are dominated by rigid forms which set off subtle changes. In the United States, lacking structure in the face of all-consuming progress, Americans have become blind to natural change unless it speaks boldly.'

Throughout the 20th century the design of private gardens and of larger, often public, landscapes has evolved in parallel, with regular overlap and points of contact. Central to Oehme and van Sweden's work is the belief that the same principles and criteria apply to both: there should be no variation in the treatment of a certain area because it is either private or public; both should have common origins in the qualities of natural landscape; and their varied treatment should be a matter of scale and what is most suitable for a certain position (for instance when surrounding different types of building).

Another challenge is the need to design gardens that can be accommodated within contemporary ways of life. Oehme and van Sweden are conscious that

much of American life makes gardens judged by whether they sustain predictable, accepted notions, are immediately appreciable, and are able to accommodate non-horticultural demands. Oehme and van Sweden's response has been to demonstrate that a garden can be both a place for living in – as advocated from the 1930s by Thomas Church – and representative of the natural landscape.

Their treatment of swimming pools, enveloping the geometric surrounds of paving or concrete with great swathes of irregularly shaped planting which remains through the year, and their introduction wherever possible of more natural water features – streams, pools and small cascades – are good examples of this marriage between the human and the natural landscape.

It is in the expression of this marriage that the garden designs of Oehme and van Sweden point the way forward. Through much of the 20th century the role of gardens as part of larger designed landscapes has been significant. In today's world of environmental concerns and heightened appreciation of the natural landscape it is entirely suitable that garden design is seen to be rooted in such origins rather than the often stylized traditions of the past. Instead of imposing a structure and then developing a garden around this framework the principle of a garden's design revolves around an initial composition of plants. Changes through the season are allowed to progress without intervention, and natural self-sufficiency from one year to the next is in keeping with a widespread desire for low maintenance.

In Oehme and van Sweden's designs, bold groups of perennial plants are used to provide a garden's form, to which hard structures, such as this white picket fence, contribute.

Part II
GREAT DESIGNERS AND THEIR GARDENS

(*Above*) At Dumbarton Oaks, as well as the large-scale garden design, Beatrix Farrand was meticulous over the planting details.

(*Opposite*) Hestercombe's great pergola combines Lutyens's architecture with Jekyll's planting.

Thomas Mawson

Graythwaite Hall, Thornton Manor and Roynton Cottage

Graythwaite Hall in Cumbria was Thomas Mawson's first major commission; he acknowledged as much by dedicating *The Art and Craft of Garden Making* to his client, Colonel Sandys. Mawson worked over a period of six years between 1889 and 1895 and transformed Graythwaite's surroundings. His priorities were to overcome the house's uncomfortable position with ground sloping away on two sides and rising to high banks on another, and to relieve it of the encircling screen of trees which prevented any views away to the surrounding Lakeland scenery.

Mawson's plans were a firm example of his idea of a garden merging from formal areas around the house to increasing informality near the perimeters. His Arts and Crafts enthusiasm for detail was demonstrated by the use of local stone for the broad terrace that he made on two sides of the house, and for the semi-circular flight of steps down to the main lawn whose shape linked the two contrasting areas, and by the oak bridge that he built across the steam flowing through the garden. Formality was continued in the neat rectangular Dutch garden which he laid out on the raised site where the original stables had crowded the house and its approach, and in the similarly symmetrical rose garden immediately below one corner of the main terrace.

As with all his gardens Mawson's attention to detail was meticulous. His own comments reveal his priorities and style of work, and indicate how the principles he followed have remained relevant. Explaining that he wished to evoke the long establishment of the Sandys family at Graythwaite by successfully joining the house to its surroundings through the garden, he

Thomas Mawson, who rose from nurseryman to being perhaps the most prolific of the Edwardian garden designers.

goes on to explain: 'The design for these grounds, which are entirely new, is arranged so as to obtain as much of the picturesque as possible, and at the same time to involve little extra labour in maintenance . . . By felling a number of these oaks [which enclosed the garden] they have been broken up into groups, and by this means many very fine views of the surrounding country are obtained.'

The transition to informality was achieved 'by the removal of some cowsheds, barns and a smithy, [and as a result] a very fine view, terminating in a rocky hill planted with Scot firs, has been opened up and is now seen from the walk which leads alongside the stream. By its margin it is intended to naturalise daffodils, spiraeas of all sorts, iris, Japanese anemone, and other hardy free-flowering plants . . . Conifers have largely been planted for shelter and large quantities of the choicer rhododendrons, azaleas and acers rose garden. To one side Mawson laid out the garden forum, a long rectangular lawn enclosed by rose pergolas supported by Tuscan columns. Parallel to this he repeated the linear design with a feature whose details have been repeated in gardens through the 20th century, a herringbone-patterned brick path planked by pleached limes and clipped holly hedges. Beyond the rose garden Mawson effected the move to informality by creating paths through the surrounding woods, lined with hedges or banks of shrub and leading to such features as the 233 m (250 yard) canal that he made.

One of the most successful features of the Thornton design was the 1-hectare (2-acre) kitchen garden for which Lever wanted a formal plan. This was achieved by laying out the square garden on an angle with the house, thereby allowing it to fit neatly inside the outer boundary wall. Mawson revealed his practicality when he remarked of the kitchen garden, 'the scheme is, of course, part of a connected formal garden, but the same principles might be adapted to many places where the details would, for reasons of cost, be of the simplest description.'

The most adventurous garden for Lever was Roynton Cottage in the Lancashire hills outside Bolton. The setting of Roynton was spectacularly rugged and Mawson's main challenge (he began work here in 1915) was to create a garden which fitted this mood. When mentioning the bridge which he built to join Lever's own garden and the large area below (which he donated to Bolton for a public park) he said: 'This example shows, more clearly perhaps than any other, the necessity of adapting the gardens to the conditions prevailing on the site, instead of commencing their design and construction with

preconceived ideas as to what is right and proper or what should be included.' Mawson built a number of impressive architectural features, in particular a series of pergolas to provide shelter, but the use of local stone, local brown tiles, and a constant rugged vernacular style ensured they would be 'free from the slightest suspicion of hyper-cultivation'.

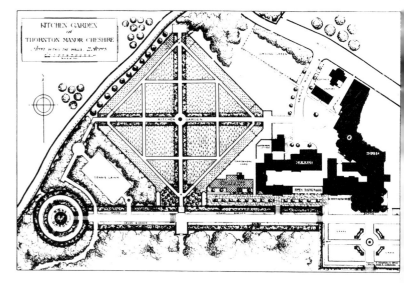

(*Opposite and this page*) Thornton Manor, with its variety of formal features such as the rose and kitchen gardens and series of woodland walks, was the most complete of the three gardens Mawson designed for Lord Leverhulme.

The planting at Roynton Cottage was equally carefully executed, with Mawson gaining considerable satisfaction that observers who maintained only the native heather would grow there were proved wrong. Amongst the main successes were 'such things as pines and broad-leaved hollies, while rock plants, among which the various saxifrages are conspicuous, adorn the rough stonework in the walls, steps and pergolas. The hardiest climbing roses have done surprisingly well, though of course the season is very late in these as in other things.' Given the challenge of the site Mawson not surprisingly considered, 'of all the gardens which have administered to my professional enjoyment, none comes into competition with Roynton.'

At Roynton Cottage, Lancashire, Mawson designed a garden whose flowing lines and quantities of impressive stonework were suitable for its setting in the moors above Bolton.

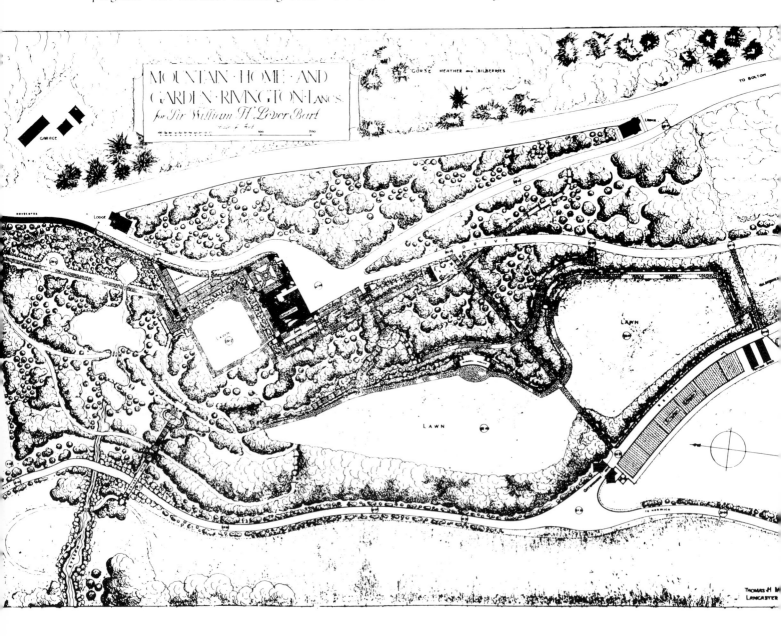

Gertrude Jekyll and Edwin Lutyens
Munstead Wood, Deanery Garden and Hestercombe

Munstead Wood in Surrey was Gertrude Jekyll's own home and garden where she tried and practised her ideas on planting. It was also the first venture in her partnership with Edwin Lutyens and set the standards for their future collaborations. When Jekyll's father died in 1876 her mother decided to return to live in Surrey and Gertrude spent increasing amounts of time there. In this period gardening and garden-writing began absorbing her artistic talents, and by the early 1880s she knew she needed her own garden. She bought a plot of 6 hectares (15 acres) within walking distance of her mother.

Edwin Lutyens, photographed some years after his partnership with Gertrude Jekyll.

Gertrude Jekyll in advancing age, in her garden at Munstead Wood, where she tried out her ideas on planting.

The creation of the garden at Munstead Wood from the 1880s was an object lesson in the development of an unpromising natural site. It was triangular in shape, predominantly recently felled woodland, with thin sandy soil. Where the triangle narrowed to a point the site was prepared for a kitchen garden. Above this the main area of formal flower garden would grow around two axes joined at right-angles, one leading to the site where her house would be built. Facing west the house would look out over a broad lawn, from one side of which the largest of many paths led down towards the flower gardens.

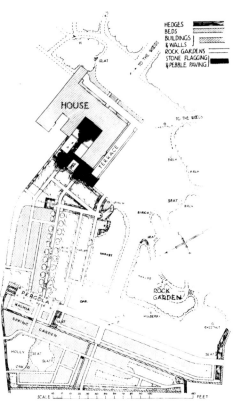

Munstead Wood: a plan of the main flower gardens (*right*), a sketch by Lutyens (*above*) and a contemporary photograph of the borders in early summer (*below*).

From the south side a smaller lawn would lead to a series of paths into Jekyll's woodland garden.

The woodland garden was built up by encouraging the best of small, naturally regenerating trees, by thinning out others, and by making a series of woodland paths each with its own style of planting. The central path was the most important and was emphasized, being of mown grass not the natural sandy soil used elsewhere. Rhododendrons were planted to flank and emphasize the main path which, like the others, led to what Jekyll called her 'flowery incidents'. Simple combinations of plants were grouped by season so that one highlight succeeded another through the year: hellebores, then aconites, and later a host of spring bulbs. As Jekyll herself explained in *Wood and Garden* (1899), which was written about Munstead Wood, she constantly planted things together for practical and visual reasons. Writing on early spring bulbs she said: 'Probably the best plan is to devote a good space of cool bank to small bulbs and hardy ferns, planting the ferns in such groups as will leave good spaces for the bulbs; then as their leaves are going the fern fronds are developing and will cover the whole space.'

Both wood and flower gardens were well advanced when Lutyens began the main house in 1895. He had already built a cottage for her (on one side of the garden) which had its own cottage garden that flowered in early summer, but the main house completed the Munstead jigsaw. House and garden fused in the north court, enclosed on three sides by the building, leading out on the other to the nut walk and other parallel paths of one main axis. These led to the pergola at right-angles which opened to Munstead's gardening zenith, the main herbaceous border. Here Jekyll first demonstrated her colour-grouping of herbaceous plants from whites and pale pastel shades through a gradual progression to deep reds.

The border, like the other areas of the garden, exemplified her belief in seasonal grouping; it was planned for mid- and late summer, and early autumn. Other areas, for instance the spring garden, came into their own in different seasons. The importance of this maxim is shown in her opening lines of *Colour in the Flower Garden* (1908): 'To plant and maintain a flower-border with a good scheme for colour, is by no means the easy thing that is commonly supposed. I believe that the only way in which it can be made successful is to devote certain borders to certain times of year; each border or garden region to be bright for from one to three months.'

The way in which Lutyens's house harmonized with Jekyll's garden at Munstead was emulated, possibly bettered, at the Deanery, Sonning, Berkshire, begun in 1901. Historically this was their most significant project because the client was Jekyll's friend, Edward Hudson, who had in 1895 founded *Country Life* which became required reading for Arts and Crafts enthusiasts. Hudson also championed Lutyens throughout his career. The site and resulting concept of the Deanery set lasting standards for the contemporary garden: it was limited in size to .8 hectares (2 acres); it was a village house, enclosed by walls and lanes, with none of the outward prospects of a country house; and it was developed on the site of an old orchard, a large amount of which was retained.

Lutyens sited the house against the north-east boundary wall, thereby allowing the maximum area for a garden. The union of house and garden is immediately apparent from the entrance in the boundary wall which leads to a paved court enclosed on three sides by the house, but with an open arch to one side leading to the areas of formal garden. Linked to the house by the architectural continuity of walls, flights of steps and archways, the formal gardens envelop the house and, as at Munstead, are arranged on two right-angled axes which gave a firm U-shaped plan. Looking from the main garden at the front of the house, a series of mown grass paths lead from the formal areas into the retained orchard whose informal openness provides both contrast and illusion of space in a manner to be repeated at Sissinghurst.

Lutyens's architectural ingenuity knew no bounds as one example shows. From the house the main paved walk appears as a terrace leading to broad semi-circular steps descending to the paths into the orchard. But the terrace is also a device for effecting the transformation in levels at right-angles to this axis; to the left the ground is higher, to the right it is lower, and from here the terrace has the appearance of a balustraded bridge and is incorporated into the water garden made through the middle of the main lawn. It is a narrow formal rill flowing from a circular pool to a central square tank and on to a semi-circular pool beneath the bridge. The orchard lay to one side of this main lawn; on the other, where it extended beyond the line of the house, were the parallel sequence of the main herbaceous border, bowling green, and herb garden.

Lutyens's architectural details gave one kind of continuity to the Deanery; equally important was the softening of Jekyll's planting. Sprays of one of her favourite roses, 'The Garland', cascaded off the retaining wall on either side of his semi-circular stone steps; the severely formal water garden was planted with simple water forget-me-nots and native yellow water iris; and daffodils and fritillaries were prominent in the long grass of the orchard. The overall effect was a triumph of scale demonstrating what could be happily contained within a limited area, a house and garden whose combined qualities were totally self-sufficient.

David Ottewill wrote of the Deanery in *The Edwardian Garden*, 'Already, at the dawn of the Edwardian age, the Lutyens–Jekyll art had reached a sophistication only to be surpassed at Hestercombe.' Here, where Lutyens was commissioned in 1903 to build an orangery and lay out a parterre, the sophistication is on a larger scale and yet the intermarriage of detail, the subtle use of changing level to enhance the framework of design, is the same. Lutyens's brief suggests sheer revival: in execution it was both original and forward-looking.

Lutyens's orangery was an early example of the 'Wrenaissance' style that he later used extensively. It formed the centrepiece of the narrow east garden where his interplay of shapes in the areas of lawn, paths of local grey stone, and flower beds – squares, circles and diamonds – overcome the potential restrictions of the long rectangle. The effect of his design is strengthened by Jekyll's planting whose repeated combinations of carefully selected plants are of a kind admired today: *Buddleia globosa* next to *Solanum jasminoïdes* and *Abutilon vitifolium* against a wall; rosemary and dwarf lavender together; santolina and china roses together; and circles of nepeta punctuated with yuccas.

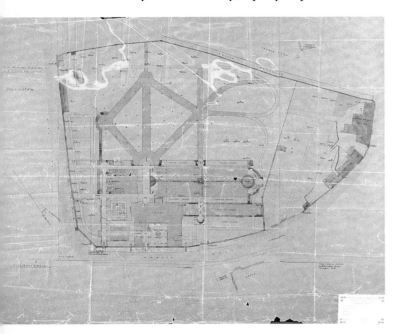

A plan (*left*) of the Deanery garden, Berkshire, and view beneath the brick-pillared pergola (*right*) showing the garden's close integration of architecture and planting.

At one end of the east garden a large rotunda pool provided the link with one side axis of the main parterre garden, or great plat, stretching away to the south. Again Lutyens used the descending terrain to his advantage. Changes in level provided the opportunity for flights of steps and retaining walls, and broke up the uniformity of the classical design: a large square sunken parterre with a high retaining wall at one end, raised terrace walks along both sides, and a sunken terrace along the far side. Here, where it was important to merge the garden into the impressive countryside beyond, Lutyens built the famous pergola with alternating round and square piers; hung with climbers it provided the ideal semi-boundary.

The water garden of the Deanery was repeated with matching rills along the two raised side terraces, each of which had borders along both sides of their long strips of grass. The sunken plat was given extraordinary vitality by the design combination of semi-circular flights of stone steps descending to broad grass paths dividing the area into diagonal quarters, the semi-circle of the steps repeated by the stone edging where they converged on a central sundial.

The planting of the central pattern of beds was symmetrical. The arrangement included delphiniums, peonies and lilies, with an edging of bergenias. But the plant combinations of the long enclosing borders below the four retaining walls were all different, depending on the aspect. On all sides blue-flowered and grey-leaved plants such as lavender, santolina and stachys were repeated in bold groups above and below Lutyens's stone walls, softening and merging architecture and planting. The blend of strictly formal design and exuberant planting was to become a standard often followed through the 20th century.

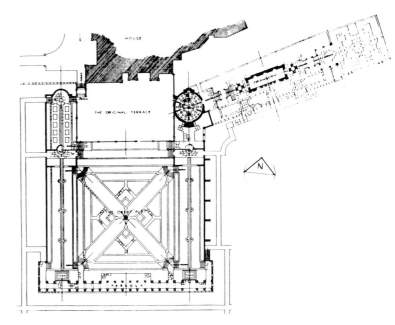

Hestercombe was one of the few classical gardens that Lutyens and Jekyll worked on together. But as the views of one rill (*opposite*) and looking down on to the plat (*above*) both show, the planting softens the formality and architectural details throughout.

Harold Peto
Iford Manor and Buscot Park

Harold Peto, in old age, photographed in the garden he designed for his sister at Wayford Manor, Wiltshire.

Lutyens was the brightest star among a selection of young architects who trained in the fashionable practice of Ernest George and Harold Peto during the 1880s. Peto's architectural work combined with his deep love of Italian gardens when, early in the 1890s, he gave up the practice to concentrate on garden design. The move came a few years after he had bought Iford Manor in Wiltshire which remained his home until his death in 1933, and where he indulged his gardening ideas with delightful originality.

Iford was clearly Italian-inspired, but it was blended into its superb English setting – the steep wooded side of the Frome valley – with rewarding care. Like many of his contemporaries Peto was inspired by visions of English gardens from the 17th century and

earlier, and he described how best he liked to evoke their memory. 'Old buildings or fragments of masonry carry one's mind back to the past in a way that a garden of flowers only cannot do. Gardens that are too stony are equally unsatisfactory; it is the combination of the two in just the right proportion which is the most satisfying.'

Peto sculpted the sloping valley side into a series of terraces with retaining walls of local stone. The main central axis rises through successive flights of stone steps to an oval lily pool. Above the pool stretches the garden's main terrace, laid out in the 18th century when the octagonal summer-house at one end was also built. Peto paved this upper terrace in contrast to the grass of the others. He carefully retained the wooded backdrop that begins immediately above, while decorating it with a selection of the artefacts and architectural fragments that he collected throughout his life: stone sarcophaguses, well-heads, and classical antique sculpture mounted on pedestals, columns and capitals. In one place he erected a loggia with columns of pink Verona marble, but the most satisfying arrangement is at the centre of the terrace where it overlooks the lily pool and steps below. Here he erected a Tuscan open colonnade with short side wings and, set out in front on the central axis, an urn on a small balustraded terrace. From here broad stone steps descend to the pool terrace.

Iford's great success was applying Italian garden-making ideals to an English setting without the repetitive geometry which made so many Victorian gardens grandiose but moribund. Columnar ever-

The open colonnade above the formal lily pool at Iford Manor is one of the outstanding creations in Peto's own garden.

green junipers, cypress and yew provide the necessary year-round structure to counter-balance the architectural features. They are enriched by spreading cherries and magnolias, wisteria and roses clambering over the columns and colonnade, and different combinations of shrubs on the successive terraces. In true Italian style Peto demonstrated that such a collector's garden depended not on size for success, but on the juxtaposition of artefacts and plants within a setting that was suitably architectural but imbued with an element of surprise.

Peto did not work as freely as at Iford in any of his professional commissions, but at Buscot Park in Oxfordshire he demonstrated to perfection the insertion of a formal water garden into a pastoral English landscape. He was commissioned in 1904 to create a link between the 18th-century house and the distant 8-hectare (20-acre) lake set at a lower level. Most of the line for the proposed water garden ran through mature beech woodland. Peto's achievement was creating a relationship between his formal water features, the woods, and the framed prospect of the lake.

From the house a grass walk leads to a quatrefoil shaped pool from which the water flows out into a

View from the house, with the lake beyond, at Buscot Park, where Peto's formal water garden cuts through woodland.

narrow canal and descends over steps and cascades to a rectangular pool. Beyond this the channel narrows again, is crossed by a balustraded stone bridge and widens into a circular pool before passing out into the lake. The larger landscape was drawn into the design by a classical rotunda sited on the axis on the lake's far wooded shore.

Neatly clipped box hedging continues the design, advancing and receding in alternate shapes to the stone-edged water. Buscot clearly recalled Italian Renaissance gardens with its sense of progression and motion; by taking a simple theme and repeating it with minimal variety; and by being sensitive to the surrounding landscape. In addition, as one observer has commented, 'Buscot recalls the Mughul gardens of Kashmir, not only in its layout, but also in being a garden in its own right, independent of the house. Its haunting beauty owes much to the still reflections of sky, trees and Roman "terms" which guard the perimeter, also the contrast between the foliage and the precise lines of the pool, surrounds, and between the pale stone and dark water.'

Thomas Church
El Novillero and Small San Francisco Gardens

Michael Laurie, an ardent Thomas Church admirer, has described El Novillero as 'one of the most beautiful gardens in the world, ranking with Villa Lante.' Church was commissioned to create the garden in 1947 by Mr and Mrs Dewey Donnell for their home at Sonoma near San Francisco. The modern house was positioned on a rocky hillside with woods of Californian live oaks, overlooking the salt marshes that extended to San Pablo Bay. The combined situation enabled Church to create a design in 1947 which illustrated many of the beliefs he had been establishing through his career.

Laurie explains that: 'He came to believe that a garden should have no beginning and no end and that it should be pleasing when seen from any angle, not only from the house. Asymmetric lines were used to create greater apparent dimensions. Simplicity of form, line and shape were regarded as more restful to look at and easier to maintain. Form, shape and pattern in the gardens were provided by pavings, walls and espaliered or trained plants . . . The central axis was abandoned in favour of a multiplicity of view points, simple planes and flowing lines. Texture and colour, space and form were manipulated in a manner reminiscent of the Cubist painters. At the same time all practical criteria were satisfied.'

The garden's central feature is the swimming pool which Church used to build up a synthesis of different shapes and lines and a deliberately unbroken unity between the garden, the sinuous marsh inlets and mountains beyond. The combination marked a revolution in garden design. The organic kidney shape of the swimming pool was entirely new and

Thomas Church, in one of his elegant Californian gardens.

positioned to cut across the immaculate linear pattern of concrete paving and redwood decking which surrounded it. The flowing lines of the pool are continued in the abstract sculpture by Adeline Kent which rises from the water to form a resting island. This combination of shape and texture in the pool and its surroundings, with no planting involved at all, marked a radical departure for garden design; albeit one only practical in climates such as California's.

The unbroken continuity between garden and natural surroundings is shown by the lack of formal boundaries. The unity is further emphasized by the way in which Church incorporated part of a group of live oaks on one side of the garden, laying the pattern of redwood decking around their trunks so they appear to grow up through the timbers. On the far side of the pool the rough hillside is brought into the garden by a group of rocks on the only area of grass.

El Novillero provided Church with the opportunity to design a garden of enormous originality, moving away from established traditions of horticulture or garden architecture. As a result the garden has assumed great significance. Equally important,

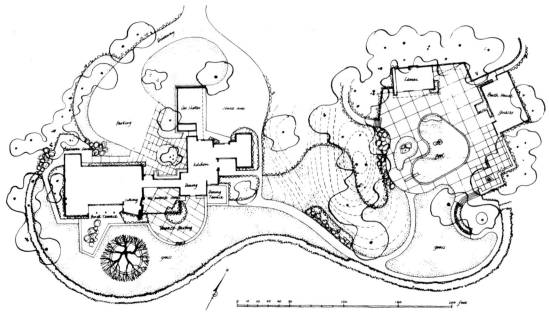

however, was his realization that such a design was suitable to the particular surroundings at Sonoma, and to his client's wishes. The variety of all his work confirms that such suitability was always a major consideration.

Among the many gardens Church designed in San Francisco the gardens of two adjoining houses well illustrate this point. The two plots were identical, small rectangles of 16 × 5 m (52 × 17 ft) and yet he achieved totally contrasting designs. The main point of similarity is that neither garden contains any grass, which he considered to be unsuitable for such limited space, the main areas being covered with hard materials. One is firmly architectural and almost severe in its linear geometry, the other employs extensive planting within the limited area.

In the first plot redwood decking leads from the house to an area of gravel enclosed by a low wooden seat, and the only planting is small areas covered in creeping, ground-cover ivy. The second garden again has decking leading from the house to a pattern of stone paving around a large raised octagon of more decking for sitting on. The lines of the paving are softened by creeping thyme planted in all the joins, and the surrounding areas are densely planted with pansies, primroses, cinerarias, small azaleas and camellias. Climbing roses are trained up a metal arbour at the far end of the garden. Most of the plants are contained in raised beds that were a regular feature of Church's designs. He demonstrated how, by lifting plants off the ground, they give small gardens an extra vertical dimension and break the line of the inevitable boundary walls or fences enclosing typical town gardens. This, and many other features of Church's work, demonstrated his improvements in the design and treatment of small gardens.

(*Opposite*) The garden that Church designed at El Novillero broke new ground in its use of abstract shapes. (*Above*) The small gardens he designed in San Francisco combined neat planting in an outdoor-room setting. (*Below*) Church excelled at incorporating swimming pools as integral features.

Beatrix Farrand

Dumbarton Oaks and Dartington Hall

Beatrix Farrand was nearly fifty when she was given the opportunity to use her accumulated knowledge of garden design and blend, in a uniquely successful style, the different influences from European gardens with the landscape of her native America. At the end of her life she knew that Dumbarton Oaks in Washington, D.C., was outstanding among her many gardens, 'the best and most deeply felt of a fifty-year career'. She was commissioned in 1921 by Mildred Barnes Bliss and her husband Robert. He had served as a diplomat in Europe, and Mildred had absorbed much from European gardens that she wished to recreate in the garden of their new home.

The size of the area alone, some 20 hectares (50 acres), made it an ambitious scheme from the outset but part of Farrand's achievement was her progressive and heterogenous design, whose principles could easily be applied to more modest sites. Her plan for the garden was in a sense compartmental, in the tradition of Gertrude Jekyll and Edwin Lutyens, and comparable to what Lawrence Johnston was doing at Hidcote at the same time. Its success lay in adapting this approach to a spectacular sloping natural site and retaining the existing framework of trees so that any formality merged with the natural landscape.

As with many of the most successful 20th-century gardens aspiring to a balance of the formal and the natural, the design was contained within two strong axes at right-angles from the house. In one direction the north vista was made, a broad series of grass terraces descending through low flights of grass and brick steps. To the east Farrand assembled a consecutive series of formal enclosures and terraces,

Beatrix Farrand, whose style of garden design integrated European traditions with American individuality.

including the green garden, urn garden, rose garden and fountain terrace. In the widening area between, the overall natural sloping landscape was largely preserved, notably in Crabapple Hill, with a succession of enclosures of different character being introduced. Curving paths of different material and pattern – pebbles, brick and paving – follow the contours of the slope, and many other details such as the shallow grass steps edged in brick confirm the gentle moulding of the landscape.

Many of the formal areas, such as the large rose garden and architectural features (loggias and balustraded terracing) introduce the French and Italian moods enjoyed by Mildred Bliss. Elsewhere the atmosphere is far more contemporary. Towards

Dumbarton Oaks, in Washington, D.C., was Farrand's most
ambitious and successful garden design.

the bottom edge of the garden the lover's lane pool
is deliberately shallow so that its patterned stone
bottom is clearly visible and it creates a haunting
combination with the reflected silhouettes of surrounding trees. The silver maples are planted in a
descending avenue to provide the backdrop in a manner that illustrated Farrand's way of integrating different areas. A curving pattern of brickwork follows
the pool's oval line, complimenting the curving brick
and grass terraces at one end, but contrasting with the
line of columns topped with urns along one side.

Farrand's most exuberant design was the pebble
garden where she reproduced the Bliss family crest of
a wheatsheaf in a flowing scrollwork pattern of pebbles, over which a fountain sprays around the edges
of a curving pool at one end. Towards the garden's
lowest level, and at a point to which paths focused
from different directions, she made a rondel of aerial
pleached hornbeams, the openings between their

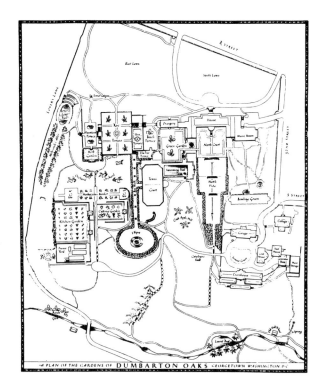

stilt-like trunks revealing a pool fed by four mask fountains. The elliptical shape suggested the garden's constant interflow rather than its discovery involving an outward and return journey.

Farrand recorded her planting in meticulous detail in *The Plant Book for Dumbarton Oaks* (1980). The mature trees that she retained such as American live oaks and beech, with the rich added variety of coniferous and broad-leaved evergreens, was a vital way of balancing the formal and natural that she effected throughout. Quantities of ground-cover plants further enhanced the garden's sloping lines, while American native flowering trees and shrubs ensured spring and autumn highlights in a manner that has been an inspiration to successive generations of gardeners.

Before she finished work at Dumbarton Oaks, Farrand was commissioned by another wealthy American acquaintance, this time to work in England, at Dartington Hall in Devon. She had already worked for Dartington's owner, Dorothy Elmhirst, and her first husband Willard Straight, designing their garden at Old Westbury on Long Island; in 1933 she began work at Dartington, which Dorothy and Leonard Elmhirst had purchased in 1925.

Dartington was a different proposition to Dumbarton Oaks in that it required limited changes to an existing garden built around the old, partly medieval hall. Richard II's half-brother the Duke of Exeter was reputed to have made the tilt-yard for jousting below the terraces to one side of the house. From her first visit Farrand was acutely conscious of the history and establishment which she determined would dictate her response: 'to allow Dartington to speak for itself, with its simple nobility of line and long human association.'

Her first change was a model of historical sensitivity, the replanning of the hall's main courtyard to give it the monastic simplicity of its original period,

comparable to the atmosphere of an Oxford or Cambridge college and to her work at successive American universities. Run-down untidiness, a central drive from the entrance archway and unsatisfactory changing levels were replaced by a central lawn filling most of the area, encircled by a broad cobbled path. Planting was restricted to a minimal use of wall plants and climbers, allowing the architecture to speak for itself and to benefit from the spacious calm.

On one side of the hall the terraces descended to the tilt-yard, beyond which the ground rose up a series of symmetrical grass terraces to woodland areas that undulated into small hollows and larger valleys. On the formal terraces an old bowling green was flanked by the remains of a series of medieval stone arches, and a lower one was lined by conical Irish yews known as the twelve apostles. Farrand's limited additions were tellingly simple: she planted a group of cedars on the south lawn; added the flight of steps from the upper end of the tilt-yard into the woodland where it curved round on this side; sited new paths; widened and replanted the border between the arches and the twelve apostles; and added yew hedges around the tilt-yard to give it more composition. But the overall effect was to draw together the hall and old garden features, and refresh them with a change in scale and rejuvenated planting.

The variety of her work at Dartington, similar to that at Dumbarton Oaks, was completed in the woodland garden which she drew into the design with three parallel but meandering paths, each given different planting. She used a combination of rhododendrons and magnolias, great banks of camellias, and more gentle carpeting of spring bulbs and meadow flowers. Although Farrand had visited Gertrude Jekyll at Munstead and was undoubtedly influenced, on her

At Dartington Hall, Devon, Farrand's work was a masterly example of the sensitive introduction of limited designs to a long-established house and garden.

own admission, by the woodland garden there, the planting at Dartington of flowering and ornamental species in a setting of mature trees is more open than Jekyll's work.

It was something that Farrand honed in successive American gardens, not least Dumbarton Oaks, where the native varieties suitable for such an informal style were of limitless richness. At Dartington it provided unity between established architecture and established landscape in a manner that enhanced both. Its example, rejuvenating rather than replacing, has been an important one for contemporary gardens planned in similar circumstances where the aim is a marriage of old and new.

At Dartington the intimacy of small paths (*right*) combines with impressive views over the terraced tilt-yard garden (*below*).

Fletcher Steele
Naumkerg

Unlike many of his contemporaries Fletcher Steele never moved away from private garden design to larger landscape schemes. Always forthright in his opinions, Steele made it clear that he would not be able to work with the committees usually responsible for public garden or landscape work. He preferred to establish a firm relationship with his clients so that their gardens closely reflected their particular requirements, and this often led to him working on certain gardens at different times over a long period, returning to make new additions as and when they were applicable.

This was the case at his most important garden, Naumkerg in Massachusetts where Steele proposed his first design in 1925 and continued working until the 1950s. In the 1920s the Victorian house had a neo-classical garden which had been designed for Joseph Hodges Choate; Steele was commissioned by his daughter Mabel Choate after she had inherited the property.

Naumkerg's name is an Indian word meaning 'haven of peace' and the house enjoyed spectacular surroundings of birch woods and views to the nearby Berkshire Hills. In the various changes which Steele made to the garden the improvement of the relations between Naumkerg and this setting was always a major priority.

This was most evident in his redesigning of the large area of lawn which extended away south from the house to bordering woodland. The view in this direction led to one of the Berkshire Hills called Bear Mountain, and Steele redesigned the south lawn to repeat the curves of the mountain's skyline. He wrote characteristically that: 'Neither the client nor her Victorian house; neither Bear Mountain nor the hillside itself wanted a so-called naturalistic affair with a path meandering downhill. A range of terraces in the Italian Garden manner was unthinkable . . . Italian gardens do not fit Victorian wood houses. The only resource was to create an abstract form in the manner of modern sculpture, with swinging curves and slopes which would aim to make their impression directly, without calling on the help of associated ideas, whether in nature or art.'

The area was graded with bulldozers into the desired sweeping shapes, merging into the woodland in a series of curves which Steele emphasized by planting hemlock hedges and prominent purple-leaved acers. Demonstrating the eclecticism or surprising discoveries which are a feature throughout the

Fletcher Steele, at work on the blue steps at Naumkerg with the owner, Mabel Choate, and her dog.

garden, Steele and Mabel Choate built and painted a Chinese pagoda as a focal point between lawn and wood.

Simple practicality produced the most famous feature of Naumkerg, the blue steps, an important example of a modern interpretation of the Renaissance garden style. Finding it difficult to get up and down the steep wooded slope to her kitchen garden and greenhouses, Mable Choate remembered that in 1938 'I told Mr Steele he must make me some steps that would be both convenient and easy . . . Little did I realize what I was in for.' Steele's design presented a descending series of concrete arches, each with a double flight of steps sweeping out on both sides, and with water descending in a channel through the arches in the manner of an Italian water staircase.

The repetition of curving flights of steps to descending platforms overcame the practical problem of the steep slope. The novelty of his design was only apparent after the scheme was finally completed.

An early sketch by Steele of the blue steps (*above*) does not have the birches which became integral to his final design (*right*).

From the bottom the back walls of the ascending arches were painted blue, and the whole staircase is flanked by groups of eerily white-barked paper birches. Their colour is repeated in arched rails which Steele added to the platforms and in the narrow curving hand rails for the flights of steps which are highlighted by dark yew hedges behind them. The overall effect is initially startling, but the birches merge the stairway into the surrounding wood, and the constant sound of water, which is increased by the resonant arches, gives the impression of a woodland stream.

Steele's first addition at Naumkerg was, as in many designs, closest to the house. Where Mabel Choate wanted an unusual style of garden room he created the afternoon garden screened by rope trellis, draped with clematis and virginia creeper, which hung between carved and brightly painted Venetian-style wooden pillars. The metal garden furniture which Steele designed surrounded a French-inspired swirling pattern of box hedging with three ogee-shaped bubble fountains, and the design was overlooked by a large bronze sculpture of a boy with a heron which Steele positioned to dominate views out of and back to the garden. The afternoon garden was theatrical and fanciful; as a result, when Mabel Choate was brave enough, after many years, to complain to Steele that the metal chairs were uncomfortable, he retorted that 'they were designed to be looked at not sat upon'.

The later additions that Steele made to Naumkerg after the Second World War increased its variety as happened to many contemporary gardens. One of his last additions was a curving wall with a Chinese circular moon gate.

Perhaps the most radical departure from accepted tradition, however, came in his design for the rose garden, which was made on a grass slope overlooked by a railed terrace along one side of the house.

Steele made three parallel curving lines of white gravel in which he set a total of eleven small, scalloped beds containing floribunda roses. The sense of movement in the winding scrolls was increased by an elm tree planted at the end of one, seemingly tying it to the ground, and by the semi-circular flight of steps leading down from the terrace.

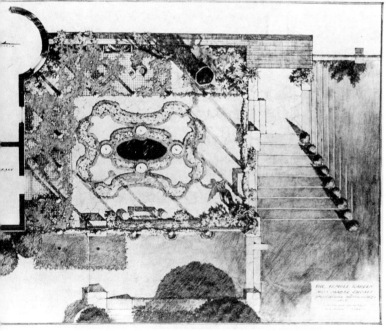

(*Above*) Sweeping lines on the edge of the east lawn at Naumkerg. (*Left*) Steele's plan for the temple garden which he created immediately to one side of the house.

Lawrence Johnston and Vita Sackville-West

Hidcote and Sissinghurst

Of all the important Edwardian gardens, Hidcote most obviously marks a progression out of the period to a new style that was urbane and cosmopolitan. Gone is the reliance on impressive architectural features such as broad terraces or balustraded walls, or the emphasis on a coy marriage between house and garden, and the comfortable Jekyllian planting. Instead Lawrence Johnston created what is best described as gardening chic. He spent his youth in Paris and that French influence is evident in Hidcote's clean formality and long axial vistas. This is balanced by the garden's most admired feature, the progression of intimate, hedged enclosures where Johnston's planting skills were displayed in impressive variety.

Lawrence Johnston and his dachshunds on Hidcote's theatre lawn, where a stand of beech trees is the focal point.

Although Edwardian in origin Hidcote moved into the inter-war period. After setting out the garden's framework before the First World War, Johnston returned in 1918 to steadily fill it out. One of the few features he had to plan round was a stand of beech trees on a mound which became the focal point of a broad theatre lawn, parallel to which most of the contrastingly intimate areas are arranged.

One of his main achievements was the transformation of farmland on a windy exposed bluff on the northern edge of the Cotswolds; there is no doubt that the need for shelter encouraged the use of hedges to provide the garden's structure. The clipped hedges, and Johnston's choice of plants – not only traditional yew and box, but beech, hornbeam, holly, lime and copper beech sometimes mixed together to provide a tapestry effect which Vita Sackville-West described as being 'like a green-and-black tartan' – give the garden's divisions an air of understatement that would not be achieved with brick or stone walls. They also provide the living quality so admired and copied.

Hidcote is in the best tradition of gardens in the way it maximizes its setting and the surrounding landscape. The two main vistas, which form a T-shape, both lead upwards to the horizon where patterned wrought-iron gates frame a great expanse of sky and open views over the Vale of Evesham. The first vista extends away from the old garden nestling around the stone farmhouse; other than this connection the garden is largely independent of the house, either outward-looking along the vistas or enclosed and intimate in the hedged enclosures.

From the old garden a path leads to a small circular launching-point beyond which borders planted for

shades of red, and red or purple foliage, lead gently upwards on either side of a grass path. At the end of the borders are stone steps up to a platform flanked by a pair of red-brick pavilions with exaggeratedly hipped roofs. They are quite different from the Cotswold vernacular that an Arts and Crafts enthusiast would have used. The vista continues through the stilt garden where the path is flanked by pleached hornbeams, to the gateway focal point.

The second axis, far longer and more expansive in scale, leads away at right-angles through one of the twin pavilions; it runs between tall beech hedges and initially dips before rising steadily to the distant horizon. At the long walk's lowest point it crosses a small stream which provides the setting for lush planting, a delightful contrast to the more orderly arrangement of the enclosures. The latter interlink via narrow openings in the hedges and are carefully sited to the garden's changes in level. The enclosures' variety of shape and planting are central to the garden's impression of great richness within a relatively small area.

The garden at Hidcote was growing to maturity before Vita Sackville-West and her husband Harold Nicolson began the creation of Sissinghurst prior to the Second World War. Nonetheless the two gardens are almost inevitably discussed together, partly because of their pre-eminent reputations, but also because they present two different kinds of gardening ideal. They share a balanced arrangement of enclosures and vistas, a comparable richness in planting, and an approachable intimacy of scale, but their atmospheres are really quite different. Vita Sackville-West wanted her garden to be romantic in a very different way from what Johnston intended at Hidcote.

Rather as Lutyens did at the Deanery, Sackville-West and Nicolson maximized the potential of

Sissinghurst's limited size – about 1 hectare (2 acres). They designed the main areas of formal garden, planted along two axes joining at right-angles, and made the open area between an informal orchard

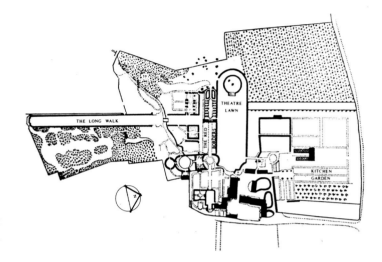

(*Left*)The old garden beside the house at Hidcote retains its cottage garden style.

(*Bottom*)Hidcote's memorable central vista. In the plan of the garden (*top*) it extends parallel to the theatre lawn and is the 'backbone' of the garden's design.

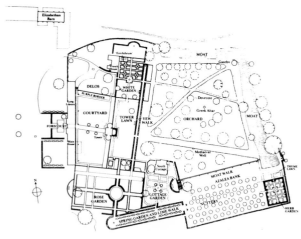

the others, and on all sides Vita's cascades of roses, clematis and other climbers covered the brick walls.

Beyond, through the tower, another existing roughly rectangular area became the tower lawn; immediately to one side of this, in front of the priest's house, what became known as the white garden was already roughly outlined; in the other direction an untidy kitchen garden was being transformed into the rondel rose garden, a geometric pattern of beds and paths around a rondel of clipped yew with entrances on four sides. The original boundary between what became the white garden and the adjacent tower lawn, and the orchard beyond, was retained in the narrow path between the clipped hedges of the yew walk. This also had the practical effect of providing a sheltered walk from the priest's house where they slept, to the south cottage where they ate.

From one end of the rose garden, where the brick wall was given a central semi-circular bay to repeat the shape of the rondel with which it was aligned, the second main axis extended first to the South Cottage's garden. Beyond this the garden's boundary was on a slight diagonal and decreed that Harold Nicolson's lime walk, leading to the nuttery and on to the herb garden in the far corner, would give this second axis an asymmetrical line.

Far from this mattering it only served to increase the element of surprise by virtue of the narrow door-ways and archways through hedges and brick walls, aligned to link the enclosures in harmonious manner. In some instances it also assisted the garden's conti-nuity. When a statue of Dionysus was sited as the focal point of the moat garden which extended paral-lel to the nuttery, Harold Nicolson discovered he could also make the statue terminate the vista from

where spring bulbs could grow through the long grass. Had this area been intensely cultivated the whole scale of the garden would have been lost.

The creation of the garden from a derelict site raised unusual demands because there was not a house as such, more a collection of four buildings: the long, narrow entrance range, the tower, and two cottages. There is no doubt that the arrangement of the buildings suggested both parts of the essential design and the various enclosures or individual gar-dens which they were each given, for example the cottage garden and white garden.

The garden at Sissinghurst was designed around the very rough divisions and shapes that existed when the Nicolsons bought the derelict remnants of the Tudor castle. The area between the entrance range and tower was grassed, its one open side walled in like

(*Top*) Vita and Harold on the steps up to the tower at Sissinghurst. (*Bottom*) A plan of the garden showing the L-shape of enclosures around two sides of the open orchard. (*Opposite*) Looking up to the tower from the white garden.

Climbing roses on the brick walls were perhaps Vita Sackville-West's favourite feature of Sissinghurst.

another angle – from the courtyard, through the tower and along what became the main mown path through the orchard.

Vita Sackville-West knew that Sissinghurst was 'a romantic place and, within the austerity of Harold Nicolson's lines, must be romantically treated'. It inspired the exuberant planting that became a model for the contemporary garden: climbing roses and old-fashioned shrub roses; clematis and a rich variety of other wall plants; hardy geraniums and other soft-shaded perennials with good shape and foliage; and vases, tubs, pots and oil jars overflowing with tulips in early summer, pelargoniums later on. Each area was a feature with its own peak: the nuttery underplanted with polyanthus and the lime walk with its rich array of bulbs, both erupting in spring; and the cottage,

rose, and white gardens all growing steadily to a climax in early and mid-summer. But equally important as at Hidcote, the continuity from one to another was firmly established by the arrangement of paths, doorways and other openings.

Perhaps the most important standard that Hidcote and Sissinghurst set for the 20th century was that they were, in different ways, entirely personal gardens, the work of owner-creators. This was evident in the choice and grouping of plants with which they were filled. In addition both have a firm structure but a limited use of architectural or ornamental features: they have enjoyable flourishes but these are never purely decorative. This, combined with the adaptable scale of their enclosures, has made them easy models to learn from.

Brenda Colvin
Little Peacocks

Brenda Colvin bought Little Peacocks in the village of Filkins on the Oxfordshire–Gloucestershire boundary of the Cotswolds in 1955. Aged nearly 60, with a professional career stretching back beyond 1929 when she was a founder member of the Institute of Landscape Architects, she was widely experienced in garden design and horticulture, and acutely aware of the conundrums confronting the contemporary gardener. She wrote in *Land and Landscape* (1947): 'Where formal gardens are concerned we have borrowed from every available source, and we have never really jettisoned our appreciation of formal design. But the "landscape" style of the 18th century was our first great contribution to the art of garden design, and in this present century the world has been watching our experiments in the free groupings of an enormously increased range of plants within the framework of widely differing garden styles. These experiments have often been more successful from a horticultural point of view than for their aesthetic value. But we are learning . . . '

Colvin firmly believed that the inspiration of the 18th-century landscape, with natural flowing lines, could be perpetuated in the 20th-century garden on a greatly reduced scale by adhering to the same principles of combination. The best landscapes were a balanced mix of three essentials, grass, trees and water, and this simplicity could easily be reduced into the smallest garden. She continued this approach, the exchange of large and small scale, in all her professional work as her partner Hal Moggridge explained in a tribute written after her death in 1981. 'These large and long-term projects have all been created on the basis of ideas developed through garden design.

A pioneer in landscape architecture, Brenda Colvin was guided by her affection for natural landscape in her design of small gardens.

She believed that each garden went to the heart of the matter of landscape architecture, posing in miniature the problems to be solved in the largest project.'

Colvin pioneered beliefs that have become widespread only in recent years, a development that Moggridge described as being 'towards applied ecology and countryside conservation as the backbone of a sophisticated design philosophy'. Her environmental fears and large-scale work while she was creating her garden at Little Peacocks ensured that it would be a haven, and its design would fit easily into the existing arrangement of buildings and garden spaces. In *Land and Landscape* she described her hopes, as well as pinpointing the problems that inevitably confront the small gardener, as follows:

'The planting is intended to give continuous calm enjoyment at all seasons, rather than dazzle the eye in the height of summer. The ground is well covered

with low plants chosen for beauty of foliage: many are evergreen and there are masses of spring bulbs. In and over the ground-cover plants are many flowering shrubs, roses, viburnums, hydrangeas, tree peonies etc, to provide flower through the year . . . I have tried to get a feeling of quiet space in this small area, enclosed as it is by grey stone walls and farm buildings. I try, too, to engender a sense of anticipation and interest by the progression from one interesting plant group to the next in a rhythm, giving definite contrasts without loss of unity. But it is difficult to reconcile simplicity with one's enthusiasm for plants in so small a garden, and I probably let plants jostle one another too much.'

The garden is less than 0.5 acre, the main area extending from the roadside boundary wall alongside the house to a collection of former farm buildings at the far end. The flowing lines of borders around the central lawn, extending in places into headlands of planting, give continuity and movement. Opposite the house an old horse chestnut provides a natural division of areas, and at the far end the stone walls provide more formal enclosures.

While much of the planting is profuse, achieved by encouraging single perennials such as hardy geraniums into expansive blocks, it was the element of restraint, the achievement of a desired effect with a limited combination, which was most instructive. Towards the roadside corner of the main area the rare silver-leaved pear, *Pyrus eleagrifolia*, grew into the highlight of a carefully selected group of grey- and purple-leaved shrubs behind a white seat which together make the garden's constantly recurring focal point.

Her creation of features on a small scale was perfected in the meadow lawn. It only covers some 50 sq m (60 sq yd) and yet encapsulates the now hugely popular ideal of naturalized wild flowers in unmown meadow grass. Anemones are followed by narcissus,

(*Opposite and this page top and bottom*) In her own garden at Filkins, Gloucestershire, Brenda Colvin used vistas and curving lines to give a sense of progression in the small area.

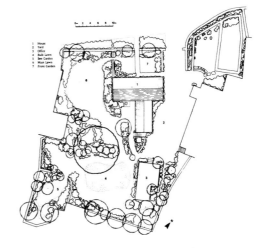

cowslips, white saxifrage and fritillaries. The grass remains uncut until mid-summer, and it is cut again before the autumn crocus and cyclamen appear in late summer. The quantities of each flower are small but the mood they create confirms the possibility of linking a garden with the natural landscape, a notion that guided Colvin's design and planting and which has become very popular in recent years.

Geoffrey Jellicoe
Shute House and Sutton Place

It was perhaps no coincidence that Geoffrey Jellicoe decided to retire from full-time practice as a landscape architect in 1973, the year after he was commissioned to design the garden at Shute House in Wiltshire. Aged over 70, his career had encompassed pure architecture as well as landscape and garden design on a wide variety of scales. During this time he had developed deeply felt ideals of design which Shute – and his subsequent work at Sutton Place in Surrey – allowed him to express more completely than his previous work.

For Jellicoe, gardens in most past periods always had a significance beyond their visual quality; they were created to be enjoyed on a mental and spiritual level. Although acutely aware of the historical evolution of gardens – which he illustrated on a huge scale in his last major commission, the Moody Historical Gardens in Texas – Jellicoe felt strongly about the 20th-century garden. Like his Arts and Crafts predecessors, he felt that it should not look back and reproduce past styles, and that it should avoid being purely decorative. He believed that it should instead be inspired by the larger natural landscape. It is a big idea and continued the long-established tradition that gardens should illustrate man's place in nature.

At Shute House the natural features encouraged Jellicoe to produce a design which achieves a harmony of garden and nature. He had been commissioned by the painter Michael Tree (whose parents commissioned his first major garden design at Ditchley Park in Oxfordshire in 1930) and his wife Anne (who was responsible for the planting at Shute).

(*Opposite*) The rill garden at Shute House, one of Jellicoe's most inspired designs, enriched with planting by the owner, Anne Tree.

(*Above*) Sir Geoffrey Jellicoe, in the garden of his long-time home in north London. (*Below*) A plan of the Shute garden shows how his additions were incorporated in the existing woodland.

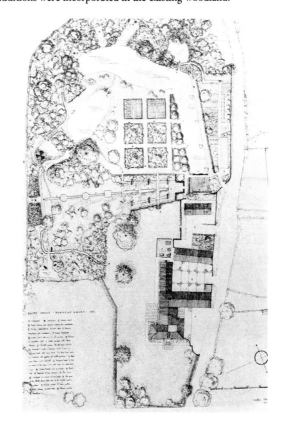

The garden's great quality was the abundance of water, supplied from springs bubbling up into a dark pool and forming the source of the River Nadder. The pool lay in a dark corner of the wood and the water fed out into another, large L-shaped pool and a smaller one before flowing in a stream out of the bottom of the wood and on through the fields in front of the house.

Jellicoe's plan ensured the retention of this enchanted woodland atmosphere. The size and shape of the pools and stream were altered; the dense woodland with Dutch elm disease was thinned and partly replanted around new vistas across the water that he created. Some of these views led to a classical statue positioned beside the water. Jellico's successful use of past gardens for inspiration is evident in this arcadian idea of classical figures in a romantic, watery woodland which recalls William Kent's 18th-century work at Rousham House in Oxfordshire. This is confirmed in the classical water feature that Jellicoe created out of one leg of the main pool, a formal canal terminating at one end in twin Palladian arches with classical statues above, a very Kentian scheme.

These changes were all moulded out of the existing features. The most dramatic changes are in the first areas that one reaches on entering the garden from the house through an arched entrance in the brick wall, marking the division between the lawn and woodland garden beyond. Jellicoe created a new water garden that flows down the slope in a narrow rill, in the upper half falling over copper cascades to produce constant chords of sound, below flowing quietly through three pools which have central bubble fountains inspired by Mughul gardens. The upper half of the rill is flanked by aquatic plants, lilies, shrub roses and dense perennials. The combined effect of water and planting is of great richness.

A simple stone bridge crosses the rill and leads to where six large square beds are enclosed by clipped box and filled with a mixture of fruit, flowers and ornamental vegetables which have replaced the old kitchen garden. Openings in the tall clipped hedge along one side of these beds lead to wooden balconies that Jellicoe designed overlooking the formal canal, and this link between new symmetrical flower garden and old woodland water garden is an important integration.

At Shute Jellicoe enhanced natural quality of landscape with carefully chosen change and adornment. The situation at Sutton Place where he was commissioned in 1980 was very different, one of the most ambitious private garden schemes of the 20th century. Despite the garden's size the scale is always human and the quality of design easily appreciated, particularly in its blend of classical and modernist features which derived from Jellicoe's joint inspiration. The gardens flow around the large brick Tudor house on three sides, and one of the most important features is the sense of progression from one area to another which prevents their varying appearance giving a disjointed impression.

Jellicoe planned the gardens to represent a journey. The variety of areas, some new, others extensively redesigned from existing Edwardian gardens, successfully achieve this impression. Immediately to one side of the house Jellicoe laid out the paradise garden, enclosed on its other three sides by new brick walls. Stepping stones lead from the house across a formal canal into the garden where patterned brick paths wind between lawn and flower beds, leading to groups of metal arbours hung with clematis, honeysuckle and other climbers. The constant sound of water bubbling out of fountains inside the arbours and out of masks set in the enclosing walls combines with the powerful colour and scent of the planting to create the desired mood. But an immediate contrast is struck as the visitor moves out of this area to the moss garden, which is a small, secret, walled enclosure shaded by a plane tree and planted with damp foliage plants.

At the far end of these adjoining walled enclosures the architecture of the house is complemented by the octagonal gazebo Jellicoe built, from which steps descend to a long paved terrace stretching back to the house and on, giving a glimpse of other gardens on the far side. Jellicoe's variation of scale at Sutton Place is exemplified by the balance of this majestic south terrace walk, and the intimate impressionist garden planted in the small enclosure against the central part of the house's south front. The bright summer flowers in this little garden – poppies, penstemon, lilies and iris – provide a medley of colour which brings out the details of the house's brickwork and terracotta window surrounds, and which is easily appreciated in a fleeting glance before following the terrace path.

Immediately on the west side of the house was an existing walled garden (which the new paradise garden on the other side balances). Here Jellicoe designed a pool garden where the geometric outline of the swimming pool is balanced by the domed shapes of planting – trained 'Iceberg' roses and low grey-leafed santolina – and by a winding sequence of round stepping stones leading out to a floating wooden island.

Outside this walled garden, where the south terrace continues, Jellicoe arranged five enormous Roman vases on pedestals and deliberately reduced the perspective along the terrace path to present a striking contrast of architectural scale. The garden's finale,

The garden at Shute contains many small details, such as this chequerboard pattern of gravel and grass.

incorporating an existing formal lily pool in highly imaginative style, is the marble wall sculpted by Ben Nicholson. A narrow path leads between dense yew trees and emerges to present the great rectangular screen of marble, its surface carved into an abstract pattern of circles, which appears to be suspended at the far end of a lawn and is reflected in the pool.

Such a powerful image of modern art integrated into an essentially traditional garden setting represented Jellicoe's innovations at Sutton Place. The close harmony between house and garden continues the aims of the great majority of gardens through the century, and shows how it is achievable on a large scale. In arranging the paradise garden, for instance, Jellico perpetuated the classical tradition and yet did so in a lively contemporary manner by combining such details as the abstract patterns of paths and lawn, and the flower-hung bowers grouped around raised bubble fountains. Human involvement in the garden, which Jellicoe knew would help overcome the imposing size, is encouraged by such details as the stepping stones across the canal from the house to the paradise garden, those across the swimming pool, and the seats positioned invitingly in the impressionist garden.

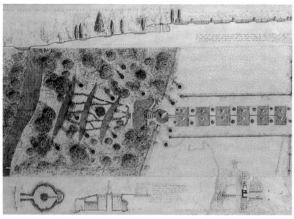

The variety of Jellicoe's designs for Sutton Place is shown by the contrast between the view past a series of Roman urns (*top*), the arbours around a bubble fountain in the walled east garden (*left*) and the Great Cascade and Avenue of Fountains (*above*).

Russell Page

The Cottage at Badminton, Culpepper Garden at Leeds Castle, and the Frick Gallery Garden

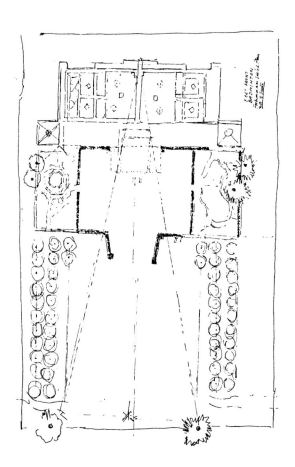

Russell Page, and his plan for The Cottage, showing how yew hedges would frame the widening view from the house.

John Sales wrote of the Cottage, Badminton, in Avon, 'the very finest results seem often to come from a combination of talents. An imaginative ideal of the owners can be turned, with the help of a great designer, into a work of art; a basic concept into a well-worked whole, designer and client each stimulating each other'. David and Lady Caroline Somerset lived at the Cottage from 1964 until 1984 when he became Duke of Beaufort and they moved to nearby Badminton House. They had become friends of Russell Page through her father, for whom Page's

work at Longleat in Wiltshire during the 1930s was his first major private garden commission.

During the two decades that they lived at the Cottage, Sales's suggestions for the garden ideally complemented Caroline Somerset's skills as a plantswoman. By happy chance Page was briefly able to help with the design of her new garden at Badminton House during the last months of his life in 1985: in characteristic style he designed two small box-hedged parterres and flanking yew hedges on either side of the house's east front, which perfectly complement the architecture and scale.

The result of his work at the Cottage exemplified the contemporary tradition of a garden which balanced delightful planting with an orderly design giving a progression from one area to the next, producing a selection of architectural features. Page's contributions were those features which gave a formal structure, not least the neat clipped hedges in box and yew which surround the different enclosures and contain the ebullient border planting. In some instances the formality was just a small detail like the tall pyramids of clipped yew which flank the steps up from the house to the main garden area, and which immediately set the tone for what follows.

On a larger scale, he suggested siting the swimming pool to one side of the enormous, ancient yew hedge which forms a backbone through the garden, making an enclosure around the pool by planting new yew hedges to the other three sides. Now the borders planted with summer perennials for a blend of green foliage and white flowers, and planted Versailles tubs make the pool area a garden in its own right, sheltered on all sides and concealed from the view of the upper-floor windows of the house.

Like many contemporary gardens the Cottage follows the example of Hidcote in using clipped trees and hedges to provide formality and structure. This is well illustrated in the combination of a rondel of pleached limes with spreading catalpas planted behind. But Page's most telling contribution to the garden (showing the influence of his residence and work in France) was the design of the formal kitchen garden, or *jardin potager*, in a style which has become increasingly fashionable. Paved paths lined by immaculate clipped box hedges lead to the centrepiece, a white-painted trellis arbour covered in white and pink climbing roses and clematis. The paths are lined with espalier apples and an avenue of standard 'Iceberg' roses, and the pattern of beds contain neat rows of fruit and vegetables.

The transformation of the old vegetable garden at Leeds Castle in the 1970s was another of Page's

This effusive combination of shrub and climbing roses, delphiniums, philadelphus and crambe demonstrates that Page was an assured plantsman as well as an architectural designer.

The Frick Gallery garden was a late project in Page's career and his treatment of the small courtyard space demonstrated all his skill in creating a picture of assured scale that would retain interest through the year.

gardens in England, and one where he demonstrated how to balance a traditional style flower garden with imaginative design. The site of the garden was uneven in shape and terrain, and surrounded on three sides by brick walls and picturesque cottages. Page designed a pattern of beds whose heterogeneous, asymmetrical arrangement matches the irregularity of the site and is accentuated by the planting; an effusive mixture including hardy geraniums, bergamot, catmint, lupins, delphiniums and shrub roses. The size of each bed and jumbled planting suggests the kind of gardens the surrounding cottages might have had.

The random character of the garden is given a veneer of formality by the patterned brick and paved paths, and by the clipped box hedging enclosing the beds along the path edges. An important feature for a garden so dependent upon its summer-flowering season is the year-long form which is provided by the hedges, and by the alternating domed clipped box and columnar Irish yews.

Page's garden for the Frick Gallery in New York in the 1970s exemplified the fastidious approach to design which characterized all his work, and which he considered especially relevant for a small city garden. 'A garden striking to the casual visitor is not usually a garden to live with and I try to avoid any trick effects . . . since even a mild shock of surprise is opposed to the idea of tranquillity which I consider more than ever essential in a city garden.' The garden originally came about through protest at the Gallery's desire to remove the adjoining Widener House and build a new gallery. The garden was suggested as a compromise to fill the site for a temporary period of ten to fifteen years; it was a measure of Page's achievement that shortly after the garden's completion it was decided that it would be permanent.

His treatment of the small enclosed rectangular space was ingenious because it suggested a much greater area and came to terms with the towering buildings on three sides. Most of the garden is taken up by a rectangular lawn surrounding a formal lily pool so designed that its stone-edging and water level are almost flush with the grass. The manner in which the water and not grass fills most of the area provides an illusion of size often found in Islamic courtyard gardens, and the brimming effect of the flush levels is similarly inspired. Page installed a simple jet fountain but with typical restraint planned for its use only in winter when there was no plant colour to provide interest in the area.

The considerable height of the surrounding walls

is accommodated by the luxuriant mixture of climbing plants whose varieties of green foliage and flowers are emphasized by the white or grey backgrounds. Again, remembering the seasonal importance, there are evergreen ivies as well as flowering wisterias trained up in narrow lines to increase the vertical element. On one side he enhanced the vertical planting by using a terrace concealed outside the boundary wall at first-floor level, on which he put a large planter containing pears to grow against the wall.

An important priority for Page was that the planting would not make the small garden static from year to year. So, rather than repeat one variety which the garden's symmetrical shape might suggest, he used different ornamental trees for the vital structural positions around the pool: *Malus hupehensis, Cladrastis lutea, Koelreuteria paniculata,* and *Sophora japonica,* all of which are notable for both early summer flowering and autumn foliage. The planting in the narrow perimeter border was permanent on both sides; white 'Iceberg' roses filling one and a mixture of pale coloured azaleas, hydrangeas and lilies the other. On the other two sides of the garden, and in the small box-hedged rectangles on two corners of the lawn, the planting changed from season to season, different spring bulbs being followed by summer annuals and perennial flowers.

Lanning Roper
Hillbarn House, Woolbeding House and Ananouri

Lanning Roper, whose gardening column in the *Sunday Times* became compulsory reading for many gardeners.

Hillbarn House in Wiltshire was one of the most complete gardens designed by Lanning Roper (in the 1960s), as against the great number where he advised on the planting of a border or other specific details. His achievement was the development of a garden with unified character considering that he worked for three successive owners of the house, and that at one point the garden nearly doubled in size. Because of Hillbarn's position in the middle of a village the garden's .8 hectares (2 acres) are enclosed on all sides and a success of the design is the enclosed variety of the different main areas; variety that was encouraged by the considerable changes in ground level.

The smallest area lies immediately to the south of the house and neat pleached limes in front of the boundary wall make an idea roadside screen, and they continue to form an L-shape along the far end of the rectangular lawn. Roper kept the planting of this area deliberately simple and limited in scale: narrow borders beneath the pleached limes were planted with spring bulbs, followed by lily of the valley, hostas and Japanese anemones; along the house terrace clipped bay trees and tubs of agapanthus ideally matched the orderly feel imposed by the pleached limes. Behind the house, steps lead up to what was the second main area, a large east lawn to one side of which Roper designed a neat hedged parterre in front of a white summer house.

In 1962 the garden's size was expanded when the land immediately on the other side of the east lawn, but at a lower level, was acquired and added. Roper made his most successful additions in the new area, a blend of formal structure and varied planting that imaginatively linked into the existing garden while continuing its themes.

From the large east lawn, steps were made down to a new path along which hornbeams were planted on both sides, and clipped to make neat hedges. Once the hedges had grown up they were grown on to joint and form a complete tunnel. To one side, in a secluded sunken area, a swimming pool was made, overlooked by small windows cut into the hornbeam. On the other side is the main area, a large rectangle of varied interest.

Reaching the far end of the hornbeam tunnel a path leads away at right-angles and stretches the length of the garden beneath a series of metal arches,

Two views of the garden at Hillbarn: (*top*) looking along the hornbeam tunnel that Roper planted to form an axial division between areas, and (*bottom*) the elegant potager planted mainly with herbs which makes a central feature in the vegetable garden.

over which clipped pear trees are trained. They continue the theme of clipped formality evident in all areas of the garden. To one side of the path is a border of shrub roses with clipped hornbeam hedge behind. On the other side is the large central rectangle which Roper laid out as a formal vegetable potager, later adding a complementary chessboard herb garden.

At the far end of the path is the most imaginative addition, encouraged by the need to screen the tennis court beyond. Roper designed a split hornbeam hedge, the lower level to one side of a path parallel to the court, the higher level stretching up behind a deep mixed border on the other side of this path. From all parts of the garden the hedge gives the appearance of being one piece and the border is hidden to be revealed as one reaches this path. The border contains a characteristic mixture of Roper favourites in bold groups; large shrubs mixing with roses, peonies, agapanthus and day-lilies.

Well designed borders were also central to Roper's work at Woolbeding House in the 1970s, where his work enhanced the surroundings of a house of considerable distinction. Ian Nairn described the view of Woolbeding's main front with a colonnade along the ground floor, looking out over a wide forecourt of lawn enclosed by walls, as 'an impeccable formal approach'. Roper enlivened the view, but without detracting from the balanced formality, by adding deep mixed borders on either side of the lawn, the planting in scale with the expanse of grass, walls behind and house beyond. Great domes of white and pink old-fashioned roses mix with lilies, gypsophila, astrantias, lavender, alchemilla and hardy geraniums, an ebullient mixture for high summer.

Designing and planting gardens to give a particularly English feel became Roper's trademark, but in the gardens he designed in the United States he demonstrated that he was equally sensitive to the

Roper's planting at Woolbeding House, Sussex, fills out a formal design of stone paths around a central fountain basin.

often different priorities of garden making over there. In 1976 he was asked to design the garden around a modern house built by Alexander Perry Morgan, set in a magnificent position overlooking the wooded valley of the Hudson River.

The house had great architectural purity which was complemented in the garden by studiously avoiding imposing Italian or French classical features so widely used in other American gardens. Ananouri's owner, Anne Sidamon, wrote to Roper saying, 'I would like a garden . . . which is not a copy of any garden style, nor a collection of passing thoughts picked up all over the world, but a garden which really fits into its natural setting.' He reciprocated these views in his initial assessment, commenting: 'Seasonal aspects of landscape are all important. Near the house there should be evergreen planting for year-round effect, and obviously it is essential for the screening of the intrusion of buildings on the boundaries and other undesirable features. However the native trees are essentially deciduous. Autumn colour, the pattern of bare branches against the winter sky, and the haze of tender green in spring are essential to the river valley. Native shrubs, wild flowers and ferns are to be encouraged where they seem natural, and bulbs naturalized in key places.'

The garden developed within these guidelines to produce a picture of great restraint that gave the background river landscape the maximum impact. Natural features within the garden, such as two prominent rocky outcrops, were actively highlighted: lawn was laid to swirl around one group, while the other, initially hidden behind an avenue of maples, was brought in by cutting vistas to it though the maples. Other than the small-scale ferns, spring bulbs and lower foliage plants in the narrow terrace borders immediately around the house, the introduction of planting was limited; Roper's skilled choices were illustrated by groups of *Rhododendron yakushimanum* used because they could withstand winter cold. The garden's most striking character remained, the view out across one lawn where a single tree, surrounded by a wooden seat, stood silhouetted against the wooded Hudson valley beyond.

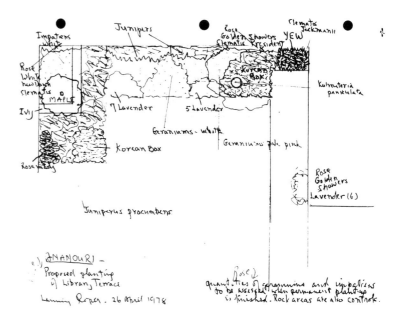

In many of his gardens, Roper's skill lay in introducing successful planting schemes into imposing views, such as this one at Woolbeding (*top right*). His attention to planting detail is shown in the plan for the Library Terrace at Ananouri (*bottom right*).

John Brookes

Denmans

John Brookes in the garden at Denmans.

Denmans in Sussex is the garden where John Brookes has lived and worked since 1980 when he established his own garden design school at the Clock House, which is set in the garden. It was begun by Joyce Robinson who continued living there, but Brookes added his own contributions which highlight many of his garden design priorities. This is immediately obvious in the manner in which the terracing flows into paths that lead out into the garden. The link between house and garden is further encouraged by the shading pergola and mixture of tubs and other containers on the terrace, all of which are filled with an abundant variety of plants.

The main feature of the garden's design is the fusion of strong flowing lines, emphasized at the joins of mown and meadow grass, grass and gravel, and around the edges of planting. To complement these features, plants are chosen for their shape and foliage more than flowering colour, so retaining a sense of structure through as much of the year as possible: perennial grasses, sedums, and herbs such as different sages, all illustrate such seasonal strength.

The most innovative areas of the garden are where Brookes has used gravel and not grass as a major medium, emphasizing both its low-maintenance potential and year-round continuity. From the centre of the garden down to a pool on the far boundary a dry river of gravel and pebbles flows along the natural contours of the site. The stones are graded in size from the largest (along the edges), to the smallest (in the centre), which suggest motion by their overall shape and flowing lines. The gravel river is dotted with a selection of seemingly random planting, spiky-leaved iris and phormiums contrasting with the more rounded shapes of euphorbias, larger shrubs, and a selection of small trees like the birch.

The overall effect of the dry river is satisfyingly natural and an ideal link between areas of orchard, lawn and planting towards the house, and the informal perimeters around the pool on the garden's edge. In the walled garden Brookes has used it to equal, quite different effect where his bold design emphasizes the formality of the rectangular walled enclosure. Gravel paths and more open areas sweep around groups of plants combining shape with strong foliage colour (ceanothus and purple berberis) and groups of herbs. Domes of clipped variegated box add year-round structure to the design. All the gravel paths lead eventually to a central focal point which completes the picture. The lines of a gravel rondel are emphasized by a circle of bricks, and they surround a large terracotta storage jar beside the sword-like foliage of *Astelia chathamica*.

(*Opposite top*) Areas around the house at Denmans are designed as outdoor rooms. (*Bottom left*) The plan shows the flowing lines of grass, gravel and planting. (*Bottom right*) The contrasting forms of a terracotta jar and a spiky yucca make an arresting focal point.

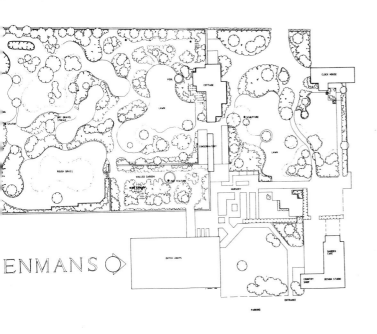

ENMANS ◇

Preben Jakobsen
Stanmore Garden

Preben Jakobsen's work is notable for exploring the balanced forms and textures of plants and hard features such as brick and paving, and their ordered relationships in small gardens. Influenced by the modern artists and designers of his native Scandinavia, his gardens also reveal clear continuity with the work of Americans like Thomas Church. There is a similar desire to equate interesting design and horticulture with the practicalities of modern life. Far removed from the traditional cluttered appearance of an English cottage garden, Jakobsen's gardens instead use plants to make firm individual statements by setting them within hard surfaces thereby creating interesting, unusual relationships.

Preben Jakobsen, whose designs demonstrate how precise detail in both planting and hard features gives form to small gardens.

This is well illustrated in the private garden he designed in Stanmore, Middlesex, in the 1970s where, considering the limited area and strong overall composition and attention to detail, a surprising number of features are incorporated. The inspiration for much of Jakobsen's design is abstract modern art, and the garden's departure from a traditional approach is immediately announced by the absence of lawn.

The garden's central feature is the swimming pool, water being a fundamental element in the overall design, reflecting the strong shapes of plants and emphasizing the garden's subtle changes in level through small terraces. The geometric patterned brickwork surrounding the pool is the ideal foil for the pebbled surfaces which merge with the bricks and the plants, chosen for foliage colour and shape more than flowers. The repeated shapes of spreading domes of alchemilla and sedums, and the contrasting wispy stalks of perennial grasses and spikes of phormiums, whose colours range from conventional variegated to copper-red, establish a planting continuity which matches the logical geometry of the hard features.

The attention to detail is exemplified in the series of small shallow terraces. Here the surface pattern changes to a geometric arrangement of brick and square tiles, and the step edging extends out to enclose rectangular corner beds. In direct contrast is the large-scale design of the high wooden pergola, which stretches the length of one side of the garden, against the close, wooden, boundary fence which Jakobsen highlighted by turning into a Cubist pattern using uneven planks.

Throughout the garden low mushroom-shaped modern sculpture and seemingly natural rocks mix unobtrusively with the planting, adding yet another dimension. The overall effect is a satisfying union of modern design and traditional planting which highlight the diversity of the contemporary garden. The challenge in all small gardens, of achieving interest and a visual picture without overcrowding, and an atmosphere of repose, is met with considerable originality. Like many of Thomas Church's small town gardens there is an oriental serenity to the garden's appearance, evident at all times of the year through the predominant permanent features.

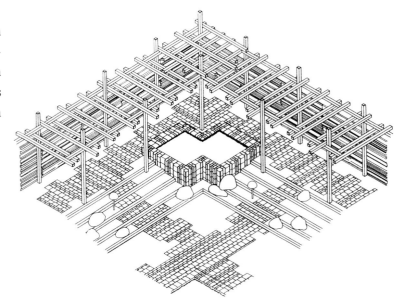

The detailed structure of Jakobsen's designs is illustrated in the plan details (*right*) showing a pergola above steps, paving and planting. This combination surrounds a central pool (*below*).

Wolfgang Oehme and James van Sweden
Vollmer Garden, Federal Reserve Garden and Shockey Garden

The Vollmer garden in Baltimore, created in the late 1970s, was one of the earliest designs of the Oehme–van Sweden partnership and it established many of their most strongly held principles of design. It can best be seen when applied to a typical town garden with a small front garden and larger area behind the house, dominated by lawn and traditionally arranged groups of shrubs. One priority for the partnership is to maximize the garden potential of the front area so it does not just become somewhere to park the car, and does not become a vacuum between

Wolfgang Oehme (on the left) and James van Sweden together in one of their gardens.

house and street. This was largely achieved by removing the lawn and replacing it with groups of perennial plants and grasses. Once mature, the merging groups of grasses and perennials, with occasional splashes of single colour such as pure white astilbes or yellow lysimachias, transformed the area, giving the house far greater privacy and a constantly changing interest from season to season.

The main area of garden descends from an existing terrace through two lower levels towards the boundary. The irregular arrangement of individual trees and the overflowing plants conceal the directions of paths and ensure that the successive areas are only revealed as you move from area to area. There is no traditional formal vista from one side of the garden to another. In one place low terrace walls are topped with wood to form an L-shaped seat, behind which are densely grouped plants such as the different grasses, miscanthus and calamagrostis, and bright yellow rudbeckia.

The pattern of paths and alternating paving and pebbles is typical of Oehme and van Sweden's use of hard features and is especially effective around the lily pond. On one side square stone paving overhangs to give a strong geometric line, on another the water merges naturally into pebbles and planting. The planting around the pool progresses from one variety to another in what has become a characteristic style: water lilies, then damp-loving *Iris sibirica* and *Lobelia cardinalis*, and singly grouped hostas for lush foliage. Particularly in the lower areas of the garden the arrangement of perennials and grasses beneath the seemingly random trees, such as different pines, hemlock and hornbeam, provides a surprisingly realistic

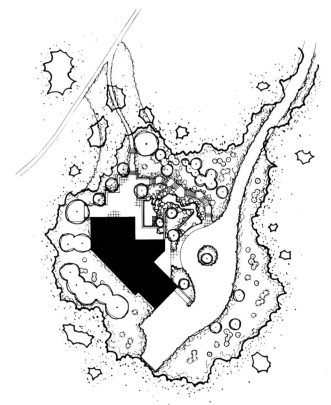

The progression from the house and terrace to the sloping garden site and woodland beyond was integral to the design of the Shockey garden (*left*). A major feature is the use of striking marginal plants beside the descending stream and pool (*above*).

From every viewpoint the dense planting of different foliage softens the lines of stone and concrete, and establishes the balance between house and woodland setting. Whether in spring and early summer, when the variety of fresh greens is at its height, or in the depth of winter when the adjacent plant groups provide only varying shades of brown but continuing change in shape, the effect is equally successful.

Most important, subtle shifts in the scale of planting effect the progression from the areas around the cascade linking house and terrace. They run from the bright-flowering perennials and medium-sized individual trees such as a river birch, to the more naturalized and scattered planting of bulbs, ferns and small woodland flowers (woodruff and periwinkle) which spread into the surrounding trees.

Part III
THE ESSENCE OF GOOD GARDEN DESIGN

(*Above*) Yew hedges give orderly structure and form a
vista at Sissinghurst, Kent.

(*Opposite*) A natural scene of reflected colour at
Wightwick Manor, Staffordshire.

Architecture and Planting

Architecture and planting are the twin essentials of good garden design and they provide a balance of structure and visual vitality. At different periods in the past, architecture has predominated to often spectacular effect, notably during the Italian Renaissance. At other times, for instance in many Victorian gardens, its application in the garden became over-decorative and not integral. Through the 20th century, however, many architectural features, such as garden buildings, have become increasingly prohibitive in cost. As a result the structural importance of the architecture of the house, and its suitability as a background for planting, have become valued assets.

Thomas Church was one of many garden designers who, however original and contemporary their ideas, have appreciated the long historical continuity of certain features of garden design. Discussing a magazine article with the supposedly avant-garde title of 'The Wedding of House and Garden' he commented, 'It is not a new idea. The Egyptians planned their houses and gardens together. The Romans knew all about it. The Greeks had a word for it; and the Renaissance Italians developed it to a fine art.'

Architecture has most often found a role in this 'marriage' of house and garden, an increasing priority for 20th-century gardeners. In the area immediately around a house the most essential feature is the terrace, for the simple reason outlined by Russell Page. 'Horizontals play a large part in all garden design if only because they can set a house firmly in place and suggest stability and repose.' The terrace has long been a fundamental of garden architecture and it is adaptable to gardens of all sizes, either being integral in a tiny town garden or the ideal preliminary to an expansive country setting. Furthermore on a sloping site the terrace prevents a garden appearing to 'be tumbling away from, or down on to the house'. On a level site it provides a firm introduction to planting, lawn, or whatever lies beyond, simultaneously introducing a variety of texture.

In the contemporary garden the terrace is architectural, infinitely adaptable in shape and size, and also answers other requirements. With the principle of unity between house and garden established, the treatment of the terrace can be decorative. You can add a balustrade; feature patterns in the stone, brick, wood or concrete of which it may be made; and even introduce varied planting whether in containers or beds, or training up against the house walls. Equally important, the terrace answers the social demands which most gardens face: being a suitable place for sitting, eating, and children playing. Today it is a rare gardener who plans without considering one or more of these factors.

Terraces were considered essential to the design of most Edwardian gardens. At Graythwaite Hall Thomas Mawson's stone-paved example, which extends around two sides of the house, exactly answers the requirement he outlined in his book *The Art and Craft of Garden Making* of a clear transition from formality around the building to informality beyond. The terrace edge is decorated with balustrading and the steps down to the garden beyond are flanked by stone balls on low piers. The semi-circular flight of stone steps down to the main sloping lawn introduces the right contrast to the rectangular lines of the terrace.

Different path patterns, stone walls and balustrading, and the pergola in the background, all provide a framework for planting at Hestercombe, Somerset.

The treatment of terraces often brought out the best of Lutyens's architectural ingenuity. At different houses he demonstrated how it could be adapted to the requirements of a particular site or the architectural style of a house. At Munstead Wood the intimate north court is a perfect composition of simple planting around sandstone paving. At Folly Farm great brick buttresses, supporting the low overhang of the house's roof on two sides of the tank court, give a loggia effect to the terrace surrounding the pool on two sides. At Hestercombe the descending balustraded terraces from the house provide the ideal introduction to the formal plat beyond.

Lutyens's versatility demonstrated to what degree the concept of the terrace as an integral architectural link between house and garden can be adapted, by shape, size and materials used. These variables should be determined by the characteristics of a particular site and by personal taste. Site will largely decide whether a terrace is square, rectangular, or has curving lines and whether it extends along the front of a house or away from it. Personal taste will usually influence whether it is built of stone flags, perhaps an intricate pattern of bricks, or wood.

Like Lutyens, Thomas Church demonstrated in

the great majority of his Californian gardens that the provision of unity between house and garden is endlessly adaptable, and can be purely architectural or combined with planting. A shading tree could become the centrepiece of a terrace and immediately suggest somewhere to sit, while a narrow border or series of planted containers emphasize a terrace's edge. The wooden decking, whose use Church pioneered, can be laid so that existing trees appear to grow through it – as at El Novillero – or be trained on supports to add another level in a confined space.

Giving a garden a simple but strong architectural structure as the basis for planting is a repeated message from 20th-century garden designers. Besides terraces the other architectural essentials include paths, and walls to enclose or mark changes in level. At Sutton Place Geoffrey Jellicoe extended a broad paved path the full width of the garden, across the south front of the house, which in one bold simple statement binds together a succession of different areas and planting schemes. At one end steps descend to the south walk as the path leads from a gazebo, at first beneath pleached limes trained along a metal-frame. Sentinel domes of yew mark, on either side of the path, the end of the limes where, in one direction, the expanse of lawn stretches away. On the other side a long herbaceous border extends between path and brick wall towards the house. Where the border ends, the path continues, across the front of the house by the intimate impressionist garden planted beneath the sheltering house walls.

From the front of the house the path continues past five giant Roman vases and leads, eventually, to a square window cut in the boundary brick wall on the far side of the garden. The path gives an immediate sense of progression through the garden's different

(*Opposite*) Wooden trellis is hung with climbers at Dumbarton Oaks. (*Right*) A plan by Thomas Church illustrates his softening of the brick terrace around a pool with trees and smaller plants.

areas and, in the subtle variation of its materials and a reduction in width towards the boundary wall window, suggests changes in scale through the various sections.

While Jellicoe's formal path confirms the classical inspiration for Sutton Place's overall design, at Dumbarton Oaks Beatrix Farrand's paths curve and wind up and down the slope of Crabapple Hill emphasizing and celebrating the natural contours of the site. Her use of different materials – pebbles, stone paving, and bricks – gives visual variety and balances the changes in planting around different paths. In one place an avenue of maples gives a sense of enclosure, in another open grass slopes are planted with spring bulbs. Preben Jakobsen's gardens illustrate how variation in the materials used for paths can be adapted to the small scale. In an area of just a few square metres pebbles or bricks laid beside square stone flags provide subtle architectural variety, and immediately suggest different plant types and foliage shapes.

For Russell Page the changing levels of a garden helped regulate different areas, and also suggested

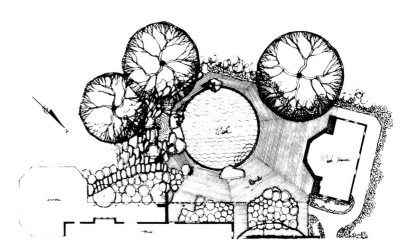

architectural treatment to both strengthen the design and provide a backbone for planting. A continuous slope, unless required for a deliberate effect, usually looks more satisfactory when broken by one or more retaining walls. These immediately give a sense of scale to the garden, introduce an architectural element which can be extended by steps, and lend themselves to any variety of planting. The required effect can be achieved with the smallest break in level – perhaps only one or two bricks' height – or by cutting a flight of stone or brick steps into a grass bank.

Throughout the 20th century garden designers have explored the balance between architecture and planting to limitless effect. Their designs, such as the sweeping lines of Wolfgang Oehme and James van Sweden's gardens, have often disproved the assumption that introducing architectural features into a garden immediately imposes rigid formality. Nothing could be less formal than the curving terrace wall overlooking the wooded slope below at their Shockey garden, or indeed in the elliptical or curving lines of the terraces in many of Thomas Church's gardens. But a sense of order is introduced that can be decorated either architecturally – as Edwin Lutyens loved to do with herringbone-brick paths or by juxtaposing straight-lined and curving flights of steps – or by planting. A line of columnar yews or cypresses along the top of a retaining wall adds to the formality of the picture, while rockplants or climbers trailing over the brick or stone work have the opposite effect.

Many Edwardian gardens, such as The Hill in Hampstead, London, which Thomas Mawson made for Lord Leverhulme, were over-architectural and presented a picture of ornamental grandeur in which horticulture played only a supporting role. But in other gardens Mawson, and, to a greater extent, Edwin Lutyens and Gertrude Jekyll, refined this to a more acceptable scale.

Since that period, when purely ornamental garden architecture has ceased to be either fashionable or practical to the vast majority of gardeners, for whom architectural features are most often considered in partnership with a planting idea, Russell Page's analysis is lastingly relevant. As he wrote in *The Education of a Gardener*: 'Garden architecture must above all be discreet. Architecturally-minded garden makers are apt to plan schemes which are satisfying and complete as constructions; but they sometimes seem to forget that a garden is a home for growing things, and that a full planting scheme, laid over an elaborately architectural framework, may add up to an indigestible whole. Architectural elements in a garden design should be frank and affirmative in their mass and weight, but simplified to the limit as regards their detail. In the average garden structures of any kind, steps, walls, summerhouses or bridges, act as foils and supports for planting.'

Lutyens's architecture is full of vitality in the sunken rose garden at Folly Farm, Berkshire.

(*Opposite above*) Harold Peto's architectural features at Heale House, Wiltshire, have been enlivened with more recent planting. (*Opposite below*) Oehme and van Sweden's white fence makes a firm line through their groups of perennial plants.

The Garden's Shape: Formal or Natural

Both Dumbarton Oaks and Dartington Hall illustrate Beatrix Farrand's sureness of touch in balancing the formal and natural elements of a garden. While personal taste may often lead to one being favoured to the exclusion of the other, it is the achievement of this balance, as at Sissinghurst, which creates a satisfyingly complete design. Whereas formal does not necessarily mean straight lines and the geometric arrangement of plants, naturalness can be achieved by the curve of a path or the shape of a plant-supporting stone wall. Where a natural appearance is introduced into a small garden, for instance at Brenda Colvin's Little Peacocks, scale and careful planting are necessary in order to avoid making the garden look cluttered or random.

The size of Dumbarton Oaks – some 20 hectares (50 acres) and the wishes of Mildred Barnes Bliss, Farrand's client, gave her ample incentive to seek a balance between the traditions of formal European gardens that her client so admired and the existing landscape. Nonetheless the result was a rich combination, notably in the series of formal terraces containing different gardens that extend eastwards away from the house, and in the treatment of the superb natural slope with existing mature trees which covered the garden's largest area.

The successive formal terraces were the ideal way to introduce a series of gardens with different character, whose variations of size are matched by changing architectural ornament and planting styles. As Diane Kostial McGuire wrote in 1941 in her introduction to Farrand's *Plant Book for Dumbarton Oaks*: 'The

The yew rondel at Sissinghurst, a formal statement that binds different areas of the garden together.

sequence from the Green Garden to the Beech Terrace, to the Box Terrace and to the Rose Garden is of great importance to the original design.' The arrangement of balustrades, flights of steps, urns and loggias, presents a complex classical picture in the form of a satisfying vista. On the main slope the seemingly irregular integration of different areas such as the pebble garden and lover's lane pool blends with the arrangement of planting around the naturally positioned standard trees.

Similarly at Dartington the series of terraces descending from the house to the tilt-yard lawn, and the grass terraces rising up the far side, present a formally arranged whole whose character Farrand confirmed with her planting alterations and addition of hedges. In contrast the woodland areas beyond demanded the informal planting of flowering trees and shrubs in groups or singly, along winding paths or around small ponds.

Lawrence Johnston's Hidcote demonstrates how the use of hedges can give a garden of precise, formal design a welcome element of naturalness that would not be possible with the exclusive use of walls and stepped terraces. For Vita Sackville-West the hedges were 'tall living barriers which do much to deepen the impression of luxuriance and secrecy'. Equally important was the range of hedging plants used, presenting the changing texture, density and colour of yew, beech, hornbeam, holly and copper beech. In addition to the hedges the style of planting throughout the garden's small enclosures made her remark it was a 'cottage garden on a glorified scale', or rather 'a series of cottage gardens in so far as the plants grow in a jumble, flowering shrubs mixing with roses, herbaceous plants with bulbous subjects, climbers scrambling over hedges . . . '

At Vita Sackville-West's own garden, Sissinghurst, the blend of formal and natural is more immediately obvious. For many admirers it is one of the garden's most important qualities. For all the regularity of the lines that Harold Nicolson planned – the yew, lime, and moat walks, and the vista from the white garden to the yew rondel in the rose garden – they provide a structured design without imposing formality of shape. As a result, encouraged by Vita's ebullient style of planting, the garden flows from one area to another with the large central expanse of natural orchard providing a foil to the courtyards and smaller enclosed areas.

Sissinghurst exemplifies the manner in which contemporary gardens can strike a balance between formal and natural instead of veering to one extreme or the other. The mixture should be determined by the nature of the garden's site and existing features, in conjunction with personal taste, and not imposed in an arbitrary manner.

Where a contrast is introduced, scale and quality of design are often crucial, as Geoffrey Jellicoe demonstrated at Shute House. Carefully preserving the atmosphere of the woodland water garden, he introduced formal features: the descending cascades and rill, and a geometric pattern of six planted squares. These enrich the overall picture, link house and woodland garden more intimately, and accentuate the quality of the woodland by their contrasting mood. Following the path along the formal canal on one side of the garden to where the water curves out of sight, greatly heightens the sense of discovery when the view appears through shaded woodland around a large pool, its edges overhung by the branches of great beeches. For Jellicoe the change was 'from the classical to the romantic'.

In many American country gardens an awareness of

(*Above*) A woodland path at Dartington Hall. (*Below*) Thomas Mawson's preferered progression from formality around the house to a more curving natural treatment.

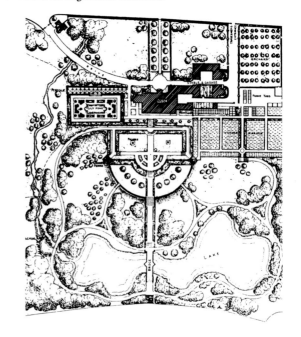

Hot reds and oranges punctuated with deep blue combine with spiky foliage to rich effect in a border at Hadspen, Somerset.

own garden at Munstead Wood she planned the main flower border exclusively with herbaceous plants that flowered from July to October because other parts of the garden were at their best through the preceding months of spring, May and June. At the same time the border showed how much she appreciated that herbaceous plants benefit from a strong foliage backing that is best provided by groups of shrubs or a hedge. However, even with the most meticulous planning a border will inevitably have gaps; Jekyll filled them with suitable annuals.

The border at Munstead was protected on its north side by a high sandstone wall but to give body to the background, various shrubs whose foliage and/or colour fitted into the overall scheme were planted immediately in front of the wall. A narrow path provided access for shrub maintenance but was screened from the front of the border by tall herbaceous plants. Especially early in the border's flowering season, when many plants have not completely filled out, annual geraniums, salvias and verbena, half-hardy petunias, and nasturtiums were some of the plants introduced to complete the picture.

Jekyll designed a progression of colour shades. At

one end she placed pale blue, white, pale yellow and pale pink with an abundance of grey foliage moving through shades of yellow and orange of increasing strength to central reds, receding on the other side in a similar manner back to shades of mauve and lilac.

The border was a complex creation 60 × 4.3m (200 × 14 ft) deep, with an enormous quantity of plants. Many required staking and later lifting and splitting. The succession from one month to another required skilful innovations. When delphiniums had finished flowering in mid- or late summer they were cut down to the right height so their stems could support trailing everlasting peas and clematis. They were grown behind for training over the stems to fill the space. Furthermore hydrangeas and lilies in pots were dropped into gaps to enhance the border before being removed at the end of their season.

Jekyll's border planting set new standards in the arrangement of plants and their seasonal display, but both changing public taste and the intensive, high-maintenance demands of such herbaceous borders made different ideas inevitable. Russell Page considered that for these reasons a purely herbaceous border was rarely as rewarding as envisaged and that a more satisfactory and longer-lasting effect could be achieved by grouping herbaceous plants around a framework of shrubs. In direct contrast to the use of a large variety of different plants Page became increasingly happy to plan a border using a limited selection of plants. Their grouping was repeated for the combined effect of both flowers and foliage, often purely white and green.

Such mixed borders, combining shrubs and herbaceous plants, were a hallmark of Lanning Roper's gardens. He had been impressed when he visited the garden of St Nicholas in Yorkshire, created by Bobbie James. The long double borders, backed by clipped hornbeam hedges, had been 'planted to require a minimum of staking' and included roses,

A rich array of foliage and flower shapes with highlights such as *Euphorbia griffithii* in the foreground and bright yellow trollius behind, in early summer at Sissinghurst.

ceanothus, and a selection of other bold shrubs.

The incorporation of roses and other suitable summer-flowering shrubs such as philadelphus and weigela, along with, for instance, hardy geraniums,

A perennial border at Dumbarton Oaks, with glimpses through to the natural woodland garden behind. The plants were chosen to enhance the garden's sloping lines.

day lilies, peonies, irises and alchemilla, immediately brought forward a border's flowering peak from late summer and autumn to early and mid-summer. At the same time pruning to keep shrubs to their required size and shape gave a border far greater permanence from one year to the next, without the annual routine of work demanded by many traditional herbaceous plants.

Long borders like those at St Nicholas, and many planted by Roper such as those framing the main view of Woolbeding House, were designed for a grand effect and detailed plant arrangements. Similarly, the famous red borders at Hidcote, where Lawrence Johnston also used a rich mixture of plants for both foliage and flowering effect, are integral to the garden's central vista from house to wrought-iron gates on the skyline.

But at Sissinghurst Vita Sackville-West wanted her planting to enhance an aura of romanticism and be ebullient rather than impressive. Instead of herbaceous plants she used shrub roses, in partnership with climbers tumbling off the old brick walls, as the primary planting elements in most of the garden's enclosures. Also the borders and beds are more compact so that the impression of luxuriant profusion is maximized.

Whereas at the beginning of the century Gertrude Jekyll's borders were planned for a seasonal highpoint, today Wolfgang Oehme and James van Sweden are concentrating on borders that have a high degree of permanence throughout the year. Many of the plants that they use most regularly, such as perennial grasses and sedums, are chosen primarily for the form and shape they retain all year round. Flowers are a secondary consideration. The constant effect is further strengthened by the use of plants in large blocks of single types instead of a complex mixture of many different varieties. This style of planting, once established, can be relatively low in maintenance requirements and is thus ideally suited to many contemporary gardens.

Bright yellow and orange rudbekias are favourite plants for Oehme and van Sweden to group for mass effect.

Water in the Garden

Prior to the 20th century the use of water in gardens was almost exclusively ornamental. Formal pools and canals, fountains and cascades added water's extra qualities to a design, enhancing a view and providing a foil to architecture, lawn, or planting. This element has continued to be important but water has additionally assumed an increasing role in gardens as the setting for natural, informal planting and for recreation.

Edwin Lutyens's incorporation of water features into gardens often showed the architect at his most skilful. This is demonstrated at the Deanery garden in the formal rill terrace he designed in front of the house. Sunken to one side of the paved terrace (or from the lower level by the bridge) leading from the house to the orchard, the rill begins beneath the balustraded bridge in a circular pool. This is half-covered by a semi-circular dome above which a stone mask drips water into the pool below. The water flows along the narrow rill, cut through a rectangular lawn, to a central square tank and on to a symmetrical semi-circular pool on the far side. The rill's alignment and the successive pools linked together the surrounding areas by aligning vistas, while the water added an extra elevating dimension to the garden. In earlier gardens its stone edges would have probably been left untouched, but the picture was given immediate harmony with the rest of the garden by Gertrude Jekyll's planting of successive groups of different iris along both sides.

Similar channels or rills flow along both sides of the great plat at Hestercombe confirming the symmetry of design while adding greatly to the overall picture. Lutyens's work in these two gardens, as well as in many others, demonstrates to the highest standards how water features can strengthen and enhance a formal garden design and introduce the opportunity for architectural embellishment. The details of Lutyens's stonework arch over the pool at one end of the Deanery rill, and the steps on either side of the other pool illustrate this to perfection. Although Lutyens's ingenuity was not matched by other Edwardian architect garden-designers, formal water pools were regular features of the period's gardens.

Harold Peto was among the most architectural designers of the period, and at Buscot Park his water garden was a superb arrangement linking the house through natural woodland to the large lake on the far side. This water garden is another variation on the

One of the two rills at Hestercombe which are integral to the great plat's classical formality.

rill, a long channel of water flowing through a series of pools. The descending levels and succession of different-shaped pools, the architectural features like the small balustraded bridge, all strengthen the sense of movement from house to the landscape beyond. While intensely formal in its arrangement the design has a simplicity of component parts; water, stone and clipped box hedging on both sides enable it to fit comfortably into the beech woodland which flanks both sides. The overall effect is the introduction of an Italian Renaissance style of garden into a natural English landscape.

Such formality of design continued throughout the 20th century accompanied by a growing enjoyment of natural styles of gardening particularly appreciated by Gertrude Jekyll. Her planting inspiration came from the countryside around her Surrey home, and the idea of a stream or woodland pond in part of a garden or flowing along its edge suggested delightful possibilities for damp-loving and aquatic plants. Extracts from her own description of planting a stream garden, in *Wall and Water Gardens* (1901), illustrate, with her unfailing practicality, how well she grasped the need to perpetuate the naturalness of a setting in the choice of plants. She wrote: 'Some of the plants suited to the running stream edge will be the same as for the margins of stiller ponds, but some that have a liking for running water will be proper to the stream itself. Such a one is the Water Forget-me-not. If it does not occur in the neighbourhood it is easy to raise quite a large stock from seed; and strong seedlings or divisions of older plants have only to be planted in the muddy soil at the water edge when they will soon grow into healthy spreading sheets and give plenty of the dainty bloom whose blue is the loveliest of any English plant. Next to the Forget-me-not on the water edge, and also a little

Vistas leading to a delicate fountain link different areas at Heale House, Wiltshire.

more inland, I should plant the double Meadow-Sweet, the double form of the wild *Spiraea ulmaria* and again beyond it, quite out of sight of the Forget-me-not, others of the herbaceous spiraeas – all moisture-loving plants . . .

'Close by the stream-side and quite out of view of other flowering plants should be a bold planting of *Iris laevigata*, the handsome Japanese kind, perhaps better known as *Iris kaempferi* . . . There are double varieties, but in these the graceful purity of the form is lost and the character of the flower is confused . . . The yellow Mimulus (*M. luteus*) is a capital thing for the stream-side; once planted it will take care of itself; indeed it has become naturalized by many streams in England . . . It should be noted that in such a stream-garden it will usually be the opposite side that is best seen, and this should be borne in mind while composing the pictures and setting out the path . . . As the stream leads further away we begin to forget the garden, and incline towards a wish for the beautiful things of our own wilds, so that here should be, for the earliest water flowers of the year, the smaller of the wild kinds of Water Buttercup (*Ranunculus aquatilis*).'

Russell Page was equally appreciative of running water in a garden. Like Jekyll he argued (in his book *The Education of a Gardener*) that too much planting inevitably spoils an already enjoyable feature. 'Before your inner eye float luscious pictures of groups of Iris and primula, willow and water-lilies and a mirage of picturesque details . . . Too much enthusiasm of this kind and you may quite likely damage your garden composition irretrievably . . . My thought is always "How little can I do?" rather than how much, to achieve the most telling result.'

As well as restraint, planting along water edges requires careful siting. Page demonstrated how the positioning of a single group of plants on one bank can have the desired effect of slowing the flow of

In Russell Page's small garden at the Frick Gallery, New York, the proportions of the central lily pool dictated the garden's appearance, but the water lilies have outgrown the limited size he planned for them.

water along a stream, diminishing the sense of restlessness that a vigorous, unbroken flow can introduce.

Page's garden designs usually incorporated formal water in pools and canals and showed the degree of elegance that can be instilled in any garden setting. He maintained that in many instances water should be introduced primarily to reflect its surroundings, and as a result the motionless surface should not be disturbed either by fountain jets or by planting. His use of water in the Frick Gallery garden in New York revived a tradition of Islamic gardens where filling much of the central area of an enclosed courtyard with a brimming tank of water gives an illusion of greater space. His restriction of the single fountain jet to winter bore out his own warning that 'The play of

fountains in a flower garden may offer an unnecessary and too rich overtone, as though a wedding cake were waltzing.'

At Hidcote Lawrence Johnston similarly evoked the Islamic tradition by filling one hedged enclosure with a circular bathing pool, whose brimming water almost overflows the raised stone edges. With only a path between pool and hedges the effect is one of sudden spaciousness and simplicity in a garden of enclosure and intensely detailed planting, a single statement and an integral part of the overall design. Among Hidcote's many design qualities is the contrast between this enclosure and the stream garden, with banks of primulas and other damp-loving plants, which subtly form the boundary between the series of formal enclosures and the natural woodland garden.

In the contemporary garden ornamental water has combined with recreation in the swimming pool.

With characteristic fastidiousness Russell Page in *The Education of a Gardener* was acutely aware of possible intrusive features and pitfalls: 'heavy ladders and cumbersome diving boards . . . Very often a scum trough runs right round a pool, a foot or so below the paved edged and the surface of the water is that amount lower than the surround . . . The surroundings of a pool need careful thought. It has too long been the custom to put the average swimming pool in a waste of paving or cement. This usually destroys the proportions of the pool itself and gives a monolithic effect altogether too large and heavy, and disastrous in anything intended as a garden frame.'

Page advocated that a pool should be designed within the general plan of a garden and not inserted arbitrarily, while contained within an enclosed compartment. The Cottage at Badminton is a good example. The water surface surrounding the yew hedges and flower border completed an enticing picture during the summer when the pool was in use, but the hedges effectively concealed it during the drab months of winter.

Thomas Church's gardens in California were made in a climate ideally suited to swimming pools, and in numerous designs he illustrated how pools of different shape and size, in gardens large and small, can either be a major feature or blend happily into the overall design. The pool at El Novillero showed the adventurous shapes that Church sometimes used, and how a pool and its terrace can often provide, right through the year, a restful foreground to a spectacular natural landscape beyond.

The linear design and sparse decoration of the El Novillero pool garden harmonized with its surroundings in a manner Church achieved in numerous different designs. Classical gardens were enhanced by a rectangular pool set in a terrace decorated with symmetrically arranged ornaments or planted tubs; the mood of a natural woodland site was left undisturbed

by a circular pool with large natural stones around some edges, and informally grouped plants to complement the surrounding trees; and in all cases the choice of brick, paving, concrete or wood edging was selected to match the site and shape of the pool.

The swimming pool at Sutton Place was one of a variety of water features that Geoffrey Jellicoe incorporated into his designs to emphasize the different character of successive areas. Each had its own purpose. To one side of the house a rectangular moat, classically planted with water lilies, is crossed by square stepping stones from the house, so launching the visitor on a journey through the garden. In contrast to the motionless silence of the moat, on its far side the paradise garden is alive with the noise of often unseen water. Here, where paths wind among luxuriant planting leading from one circular bower to another, water's sound is its main quality. The visual appearance is deliberately restrained to bubbling bowl fountains in the centre of each bower, and stone masks hidden along the garden's side walls. The swimming pool itself is integrated into the walled garden by roses and domes of clipped santolina surrounding the low retaining wall that rises from the pool's stone surround.

Finally, the garden's climax is the view of Ben Nicholson's huge white marble wall sculpture reflected in a formal lily pool in front. Jellicoe's most ambitious water design for Sutton Place, a long cascade descending to a pool and underground grotto, was never executed, but the other features well illustrate how water can be introduced to compliment different designs in the contemporary garden.

Intriguingly different was the situation of Shute House where limitless quantities of natural water provided the whole mood and *raison d'être* of the garden. Jellicoe's achievement was to introduce new water features: the canal, cascades, and rill which enlivened the garden's overall appearance while retaining the

Swimming pools at Sutton Place by Geoffrey Jellicoe (*above*) and in a California garden by Thomas Church (*below*).

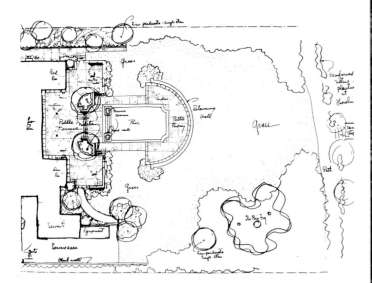

completely undisturbed nature of the woodland pool and spring.

The Shute House garden demonstrated how water can equally influence a garden's mood as its appearance. For this and other reasons, like the danger

At Vann, Surrey, a pool feeds a stream whose banks were originally planted by Gertrude Jekyll with bulbs and meadow flowers.

of being out of scale or proportion to other garden features, successive 20th-century designers have advocated water features that are bold but unfussy and carefully chosen for their particular surroundings. A formal pool can be ruined when surrounded by complicated, colourful planting, or by the constant distraction of an inappropriate fountain. Similarly a woodland stream can be transformed from a scene of undisturbed nature to artificiality by an over-abundance of colourful waterside plants.

Despite such potential dangers the contemporary

A detail of one of Geoffrey Jellicoe's 'musical' cascades in the rill at Shute House, Wiltshire.

garden has successfully explored the integration of water in a more widely varied manner than was true in the past. That the integration is often on a reduced scale does not lessen the impact if a scheme is well executed. As Fletcher Steele showed with the blue steps at Naumkerg, if a surprise element is desired, nothing has a more immediate and telling impact than water – something which is of particular relevance in small gardens.

Garden Ornament

Arts and Crafts enthusiasts criticized Victorian gardens for their over-decoration. Ornaments were used primarily for decorative effect and to give an appearance of richness and grandeur instead of being in harmony with the whole design. The result was a bewildering array of urns, statues, loggias, and fountains vying for attention with each other and bright parterres. It was a product of Victoriana combined with the fashion for Italianate gardens. But while the Italian influence continued into the Edwardian period and later 20th-century gardens, leading designers began treating ornaments within a garden's overall context rather than simply as a means of dutifully recreating the past.

Thomas Mawson's elevation and plan for a scheme of ornamental trellis work.

By contrast the inspiration for the Arts and Crafts garden was, in a sense, more domestic. Jane Brown hinted as much in her analysis of an imaginary Arts and Crafts garden in her book *The English Garden in our Time* (1987): 'the ideal Arts and Crafts garden surrounds its Edwardian vernacular house, and is laid out so that straight paths and vistas spring from the house doors and windows. Both house and paths are bordered with flowers, and the paths are of stone and brick, sprouting thrift and thymes, leading to yew-walled rooms furnished with a sundial or a pool and a seat for contemplation. Somewhere one walks between a pergola, dripping with wisteria or laburnum, to a small summerhouse . . . '

These priorities had the all-important effect of giving a human scale to garden ornaments. They should

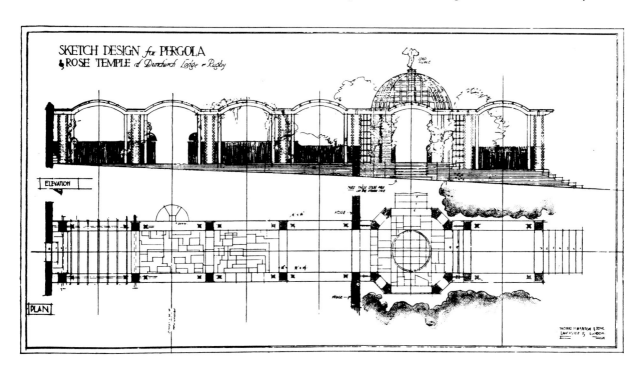

be enjoyable but not overwhelming. The close link between house and garden suggested that ornament would be most satisfying when used to complement the architectural style of a house, continuing it into the garden, repeating details or providing a foil for planting. This was exemplified in Gertrude Jekyll and Edwin Lutyens's gardens, where the architect's unfailing originality was always evident. A succession of gardens demonstrate his flair for providing ornament in the detail or finish of architectural features such as steps, walls, and pools, and nowhere better than the Deanery garden. The patterns of stone flags and narrow tiles in the square or semicircular flights of steps; the balustrade along the raised terrace or bridge with its bold, distinctly Tudor, pattern of stone arches; and the pattern of the domed roof over the pool at one end of the formal rill all strengthen and enrich the Deanery garden's structure and appearance.

Details at Hestercombe are similarly satisfying, especially in the combination at the end of one of the rills. The stone-lined rill leads to a slightly sunken pool beneath an arched roof set in a stone wall with a balustrade. Circular stone lunettes are set in the wall on either side, and beyond these the flanking walls sweep down in great curves. The only purely ornamental decoration in the design is the stone mask on the central keystone of the pool's domed roof. And yet the decorative effect of integrated patterns of stonework, the alternating golden Bath stone and grey Ham stone, is enormously effective.

Lutyens's ornamental detailing was equally well suited to the intimate Arts and Crafts-inspired gardens of his partnership with Jekyll, and to the grander classical gardens of his later career. Through the Edwardian period and on into the later 20th century

A classical statue completes a formal scheme at Godinton Park, Kent. The gardens were originally laid out in the 18th century and further extended by Sir Reginald Blomfield.

the continuing admiration of the Italian garden style has been among the strongest incentives for the integration of ornament into gardens. The change from the Victorian/Italianate grandeur of, for instance, gardens by Charles Barry, is perfectly demonstrated at Harold Peto's Iford Manor. The steeply sloping site was ideally suited to a terraced, Italian garden. More significant, Peto had long been a collector of classical architectural details, antiquities and sculpture, and their display was central to the garden's design. And yet, because Peto incorporated the terraced design and his array of ornaments, into the existing landscape, and balanced them with planting along the terraces, the garden never gives the impression of being imposed or a pastiche.

The terraces are linked by a vista of successive flights of stone steps between elegant piers, surmounted with lead urns or columns topped by pairs of figures or animals. The broad upper terrace that stretches across the garden is most richly decorated, the seemingly heterogeneous collection of colonnades, columns, statues, well-heads and other pieces disguising their skilful arrangement and harmonizing with the flanking trees. Elsewhere walls a•e decorated with stone panels or figures, and the whole is a vibrant descendant of an Italian baroque garden.

Peto's display of garden ornament was primarily decorative but worked because the overall design was on a manageable scale, and because of the arrangement of the different features in relation to each other and the garden's planting. The requirement for ornamental features to be an integral part of a garden's design was paramount in many other gardens. In an essentially horticultural garden such as Hidcote, the few ornamental features Lawrence Johnston introduced are impeccably effective and it is impossible to imagine the garden without them. This is especially true of the ornamental gateways at the end of the garden's two main vistas, opening symbolically onto the countryside and views beyond, and the detailing of the delightful hipped roofs of the twin gazebos between the red borders and stilt garden, through which the two vistas pivot at right-angles.

Where Johnston moulded Hidcote's ornamental features into the garden's overall design, at Sissinghurst Vita Sackville-West and Harold Nicolson positioned classical statues at the focal points of the garden's main vistas and placed terracotta urns, oil jars and other containers – all filled with seasonal flowers – to emphasize the abundance of the garden's planting. Ornament, design and planting joined together to strengthen the overall picture, whether in the views across the orchard and along the moat walk to the figure of Dionysus on the far side of the moat, or to the planted oil jar in the centre of the white garden.

The use of ornaments in partnership with planting has been of abiding importance for 20th-century designers and his enabled gardens such as Sissinghurst to greatly enhance their appearance for more than decorative reasons. This partly explains the popularity of pergolas in Edwardian gardens, whose framework of brick or stone and wood was hung with climbing plants, and of the wooden trellises that have adorned gardens throughout the 20th century. An ideal example was the white-painted wooden arbour that Russell Page designed as the central feature of the formal kitchen garden at the Cottage in Badminton, hung with climbing roses and solanum, completing the pattern of box-edged planting and neat paths.

Strengthening a garden's design and the effect of planting have been important uses of ornament in the contemporary garden. So too has been the achievement of bold statements and occasional surprises. At Sutton Place the great marble wall by Ben Nicholson that Geoffrey Jellicoe planned as the garden's finale is just such a statement. In the same garden the line of

Roman urns that he displayed to one side of the main path immediately change the garden's scale by their huge size. Jellicoe's designs have skilfully balanced the classical tradition that be upholds, and which is illustrated in simple form by his positioning of an elegant Italian statue as the focal point of the descending cascade and rill at Shute House. It is also evident in his enthusiasm for abstract modern art – notably Nicholson's wall – which in the right garden setting can be used to great effect.

Abstract art and new materials for garden ornaments have been two influences behind the temptation to experiment with shape and form. Hence the use of metal and man-made structures. But designers have shown that the desire to be adventurous should always be tempered by what is suitable for a particular garden site and its scale. In a large garden with a varied composition, such as Dumbarton Oaks, a bold ornamental statement like the pebble garden with its Italianate fountain and intricate patterning are features of exciting individuality that do not disturb the garden's overall scale and composition. Equally important, as Thomas Church often stressed, an ornament like a statue or abstract sculpture can provide year-round constancy in a scene of seasonally changing plant appearances. This sense of permanence can be disturbed if the size and material of the ornament do not blend easily with its surroundings.

Most designers advocate that ornament is best used to enrich a garden's overall appearance, not for individual display. In the case of furniture the priority should be to combine what might be a fine ornamental feature with maximum human enjoyment of the garden. So a seat is of little use, however impressive it appears, if uncomfortable or badly positioned in an unsheltered position offering a poor outlook.

(*Opposite top*) The Nicholson wall at Sutton Place. (*Opposite bottom*) One of the planted copper pots that Vita Sackville-West put at focal points at Sissinghurst.

Beatrix Farrand's pebble garden at Dumbarton Oaks has an exuberant mixture of swirling patterns, a fountain basin at one end and trellis surround hung with climbing plants.

Although it is hard to imagine the ever-bustling Gertrude Jekyll ever sitting in her own garden, Munstead Wood had a number of seats carefully positioned to give the most rewarding views of different areas. The wooden seat Lutyens designed, in his now familiar pattern of curving back and arms, for the secluded north court was an ideal example. Set against the house's wall, beneath the overhanging upper floor, the seat looked out across the neat planting and paving of the court to the larger garden beyond, combining an invitation to rest with another to explore. At Dumbarton Oaks, where the sloping terrain in one place suggested creating steps leading

from the north end of the wooded walk known as Melissande's allee, Beatrix Farrand designed a slightly curving retaining stone wall in the bank with simple flights of steps curving down on either side. She also positioned a wide wooden seat with lattice-patterned back panels in front of the wall, protected by the bank and looking out across the sloping garden.

Emphasizing the link between house and garden in details such as patterned brick and stonework, strengthening a garden's design by giving focal points to vistas and a decorative element to architectural structure, providing planting with either a setting (like an urn) or a foil (statue or sculpture), and bringing permanence to a garden's scale through the year, have all become key ways of using ornament in the contemporary garden.

Expense is another consideration, all too often limiting a gardener's choices. But the repeated message from garden designers is that ornament, whether costly or affordable, should be used in a garden in relation to its other component parts, and not imposed arbitrarily in the hope of adding an air of sophistication. Given the huge array of sculptural forms, materials, and different garden styles that have developed since the Victorian stereotypes, ornament is potentially one of the most rewarding features of the garden. Yet as the creators of Victorian gardens were apt to forget, a little usually goes a long way, and a striking effect can often be gained with the lightest touch.

(*Opposite*) A Henry Moore sculpture overlooks the 600-year-old tilt-yard garden at Dartington Hall. (*Above*) The stone sculpture of a boy gives warm animation to the garden of Denmans, Sussex.

Hedges, Trees and Shrubs

There are many fine 20th-century gardens that rely purely on hedges, and carefully sited trees and shrubs for their structural form in addition to a large degree of visual interest. The cost of highly architectural, formal gardens dependent upon walls and terracing for their composition began to be prohibitive at the same time as the Arts and Crafts movement was advocating a warmer, more human style of garden. These two factors combined to promote the use of hedges so that by the turn of the century even a firm advocate of formal, architectural gardens such as Reginald Blomfield used clipped hedges, usually yew, as a key part of his major garden designs.

Blomfield's championing of yew reflected the views of his contemporaries, and indeed of future garden designers. Gertrude Jekyll's characteristically succinct summary of yew's quality as hedging plant remains as true today as when written over 80 years ago in *Gardens for Small Country Houses* (1912) co-authored by Lawrence Weaver: 'Compared with the yew no other tree is so patient of coercion, so protective in its close growth, or so effective as a background to the bright bloom of parterre or flower-border. Its docility to shaping into wall, niche, arch and column is so complete and convenient that it comes first among growing things as a means of expression in that domain of design that lies between architecture and gardening.'

The writer Osbert Sitwell once remarked that his

Clipped yew hedges terminating in tall pyramids provide the major framework for the garden at Renishaw.

turn-of-the-century childhood seemed to develop at the same annual pace as the yew hedges his father had planted to divide the terraced enclosures of his Italian garden at their Renishaw home in Derbyshire. Long borders backed by yew hedges and neat enclosures or

protective boundaries of yew were hallmarks of the Edwardian garden. Thomas Mawson's battlemented hedge along one boundary and his neat little yew-hedged Dutch garden at Graythwaite Hall were typical. In the same garden his choice of trees and shrubs for the perimeters well illustrated how he planned to effect a transition from garden to countryside. The terraces, rose garden and neat lawns lead away to the stream garden whose far bank was adorned with groups of azaleas, rhododendrons and acers; further beyond, beech and ornamental conifers were planted among the native Scots pine and oaks.

At Thornton Manor Mawson's planting similarly bound together the garden and its bordering woodland. He laid out walks leading from the far end of the garden into woodland, lining them either with hedges or banks of shrubs.

At Dartington Hall Beatrix Farrand planted yew hedges very effectively around the ends of the garden's focal open area, called the tilt-yard. Sunken below terraces on both sides, the tilt-yard is the hub of Dartington and the hedges formalized its open space. Elsewhere at Dartington Farrand's choice of trees and shrubs demonstrated her skill at building up a variety of scenes. In the hall's courtyard where she aimed at tranquil simplicity, she limited new planting of the open lawn area to four flowering *Prunus* × *yedoensis*. Beyond the head of the tilt-yard she cleared the undergrowth from a bowl-like depression with a small pool and planted an azalea dell. In the woodland that swept along banks above the tilt-yard on two sides she removed undergrowth and banks of laurel to open up views through the mature oaks, ilex and beech, and created a series of paths at different levels, each with its own particular planting, the selection of which was carefully controlled. 'The lower one was flanked by magnolias and rhododendrons,' she explained, 'the colour range being strictly limited to ivory and blue, with a touch of pink, in order to bring out rather than overshadow, the Davidia and magnolias.'

Farrand's skilful selection and siting of the different varieties of ornamental and flowering trees and shrubs transformed the overgrown Dartington woodland into a coherent design with a clear seasonal progression. At Dumbarton Oaks her work was similarly attentive, addressing different areas both in terms of their individual requirements and as part of the whole garden. The siting of a tree or group of trees could, in the case of the long north vista from the house, frame the view and simultaneously provide the link to areas of the garden beyond.

Farrand's own description of the planting of two different areas of the garden reveal her guiding priorities. Explaining her choice of planting along the east lawn she wrote in *The Plant Book for Dumbarton Oaks*: 'following the walk eastward from the gatehouse on the south side of the lawn the groups are composed of *Pieris japonica*, Oregon grape *(Mahonia aquifolium)*, a magnificent Katsura tree *(Cercidiphyllum japonicum)* and an equally fine Japanese maple *(Acer palmatum)*. These trees and shrubs make a foliage border to the lawn difficult to equal for character and delicacy. The old plants, such as the Cercidiphyllum and the Japanese maples, were growing in these places when the land was acquired by Mr and Mrs Bliss. The new planting has been made in an effort to bring out these beautiful old plants and yet given an additional evergreen screen where the Cercidiphyllum and the Maple are bare in winter. Therefore American holly, English holly, Oregon grape and Japanese holly, have been used in this border.'

Of Crabapple Hill she wrote: 'But the hillside itself should be kept to a comparatively few sorts of Crab apples . . . Too much of a variety is not likely to be successful, as the attractiveness of this part of the design should consist of the mass of flowering trees in the early season – each one having at least enough

room to develop adequately, if not completely – and the hanging fruits in the autumn.'

One of Farrand's most successful designs at Dumbarton Oaks was the box rondel (later replaced with clipped hornbeams) which created a tranquil enclosure around the lawn and a central pool. The design illustrated Russell Page's view when he wrote in *The Education of a Gardener*: 'I think of hedges as enclosures, and it is with hedges that you may best articulate the bony structure, the skeleton as it were, of a garden. For this a hedge should usually be close in texture, monotone in colour and sharply defined in shape. I would therefore restrict myself to the classic materials: on box and yew, holly, ilex and bay laurel, beech and hornbeam, cypress, pittosporum, myrtle, lavender and rosemary.'

Page was writing about gardens in many countries and a number of the plant varieties he lists, such as pittosporum and myrtle, are not reliably hardy in most areas of Britain. But in another passage he concisely described an example which confirmed how hedges create a living framework. During the 1930s he and Geoffrey Jellicoe worked in partnership, and watching Jellicoe work at his most important pre-war commission at Ditchley Park, Page noted in the same book: 'It was from Geoffrey Jellicoe that I learned how important this could be – by watching the progress of his work at James Gibbs's domestic masterpiece, Ditchley Park. Here he established the relationship between house and landscape by extending its main facade with long ten-foot high beech hedges which back a long grass terrace. This was enough to "place" the house firmly in its setting and make a starting-point for a series of enclosed gardens to match the stateliness of the architecture.'

'How seldom one sees a tapestry hedge, that subtle civilization of the wild hedgerow,' Page wrote on another occasion. At Hidcote he would be able to enjoy a tapestry hedge as one feature of a garden

where hedges were planted to masterly effect. Forming enclosures, backing borders and flanking orderly vistas, the hedges were clipped to a thickness and height which were in scale with their particular situation.

Their plants were chosen to be similarly suitable. From the 'old garden' beside the Hidcote house borders Lawrence Johnston planted a border leading to the circle, a setting-off point with paths going out at right-angles enclosed by yew hedges clipped low enough to allow enticing views to the parts of the garden on different sides. Next along the main vista from the house, the red borders are also backed by yew but, as Vita Sackville-West noted in her weekly *Observer* column: 'There is a great deal of yew, but Major Johnston has not been content with plain yew, skilfully as he employed it. In one place there is a

Varied effect of a tapestry copper beech and holly hedge and low clipped box at Hidcote.

mixed hedge of yew and box, an attractive combination with its two shades of green: he has realized how many different shades of green there are in Nature, not forgetting the value of dark pools of water with their *chatoyant* reflections, and he has made use of all these greens in a way that would have delighted Andrew Marvell. Different textures of leaf have also been made to play their part, in the "flatness" of yew contrasted with the interplanted shine of holly. Then there is one harlequin of a hedge with five different things in it; yew, box, holly, beech and hornbeam.'

Although the early growing stages of hedges, when they are too small to provide real structure can be frustrating, one of their attractions is the manner in

which they grow with a garden, maturing in size and shape in harmony with a border planted in front, or steadily achieving the desired height to make a secluded enclosure. This sense of growing to fulfil a function is also true of trees and shrubs planted for ornamental effect, to screen a boundary or make a focal point in a garden. Successive garden designers have shown how, whether in a woodland setting or a formal, classical garden, the choice of a tree for its appearance, eventual size and shape, is of paramount importance. As Beatrix Farrand suggested for her treatment of Crabapple Hill at Dumbarton Oaks, keeping a combination of trees and shrubs simple by limiting the different varieties used almost invariably presents a more satisfying picture than a group of bewildering variety. When some variety is desired, for instance in a bold group of shrubs, the repetition of one plant with strong form and foliage through the group often provides the necessary sense of unity.

At Ananouri, Lanning Roper planned the main view from the house across open lawn to the panorama of the wooded Hudson valley. His retention of a single maple tree near the centre of the lawn, its lower branches clipped so as not to obscure the view, its spreading canopy shading a seat below, exemplified the impact a single tree can have when either planted for this purpose or given free rein. In such a situation a single tree, or possibly a small group of one variety, assumes the quality of statuary in a manner that has become an important feature of 20th-century garden design. Columnar trees such as Lombardy poplars, fastigiate beech, or Italian cypresses can frame a vista as effectively as the pillars of a gateway, while the siting of a single tree on an expanse of lawn, as at Ananouri, almost demands the positioning of a seat in the shade below.

In addition to making statements within a garden, providing single ornamental features of year-round importance, trees and shrubs have provided garden designers with the means of achieving harmony between the classical, architectural styles of the past, and the wooded, natural ideal of the present. At both the Deanery garden and Sissinghurst the juxtaposition of a large, open orchard with small-scale, formally arranged areas – at the Deanery with a high degree of architectural detail, and at Sissinghurst within the pattern of hedged vistas and walled enclosures – exactly expresses this harmony.

Even within a relatively small garden it is possible to achieve a natural atmosphere through the appropriate choice and positioning of trees. At Denmans John Brookes has planted so that beyond the main borders grass paths wind among singly grouped varieties of trees, such as silver birches, eventually leading to a pool by the garden's edge resembling a woodland pond.

As the range of trees and shrubs commercially available has expanded constantly, so too has their influence. Ornamental flowering or foliage trees might only be at their best for a few weeks, but the evergreens are constant through the year and, like hedges, can contribute to a garden's sense of unity. The one factor which has largely accounted for their increasing importance in 20th-century gardens was pinpointed by Thomas Church. 'In the intimate and humanized landscape trees become the greatest single element linking us visually and emotionally with our surroundings . . . It's no wonder that when we first think of a garden we think of a tree . . . The right tree provides instant serenity - something, in this modern world, which cannot be cherished too highly.'

(*Opposite*) At Buscot Park, Oxfordshire, the descending series of yew hedges frames the view to the gate piers in the distance and invites exploration into the areas between them.

Flowering cherries in the orchard at Sissinghurst (*left*), a delicate small acer in Brenda Colvin's garden at Filkins (*above*) and the trunks of birches at Denmans (*below*).

The Small Garden

The concept of a small garden has changed quite dramatically through the present century. Most of the places featured in *Gardens for Small Country Houses*, written by Gertrude Jekyll and Lawrence Weaver, would today be generally considered country house gardens of impressive size and character. Then they were small in comparison with the past. A garden like the Deanery is a good example. It illustrated what could be made of an enclosed village site with no outward links to the adjoining countryside and it had to be planned within existing boundaries. Although complex the design maximized the site's potential. It demonstrated how in a restricted space variety can be incorporated by the arrangement of paths and vistas, and by minute attention to detail, whether in Jekyll's planting of Lutyens's architectural features. It also showed how the intrinsic bond between house and garden can take away the urge for a link with the outside world.

In design terms the move towards smaller gardens was often a matter not just of size but of scale. Seclusion and the owner's personality became the hallmarks; it was in marked contrast to the expansive displays of the Victorians.

The division of a garden into a series of rooms emerged at a time when harmony between house and garden was of paramount importance and immediately assisted this union. Dividing a large area into a series of enclosures, perhaps linked by views through gateways or openings in hedges, introduced a sense of intimacy, even secrecy, as to what lay beyond, as well as continuity from area to area.

Equally important the idea of garden room fits in with the great variety of 20th-century gardens.

Different styles of planting – perhaps for successive seasons – or the introduction of an area with a formal, architectural emphasis, could be achieved with a series of different compartments. Nowhere has this been achieved in more celebrated fashion than at Hidcote where each hedged enclosure presents its own horticultural picture.

In addition to the high quality of each enclosure Hidcote continued the design principle exemplified by Jekyll and Lutyens at Deanery garden; effectively juxtaposing areas or rooms of contrasting scale and size. Such sub-division provided a more intimate human scale that has since become very popular. Taking up the Hidcote 'theme' – a series of rooms leading away from the house to the garden's dramatic vistas along the red borders and the long walk – Beatrix Farrand gave Dumbarton Oaks a series of terraced garden rooms on one axis, here providing a progressive introduction to the more open areas of naturally planned garden beyond.

The garden room has been a theme of ever-increasing relevance through the 20th-century, enabling designers to present the variety of planting and architectural style in an orderly, enjoyable manner. Initially reducing the scale of large or medium-size gardens, it has been equally significant by laying the foundations for the design of small contemporary gardens where integrating many features in one limited space is necessary. Today such a garden is likely to be an urban space of a few square metres, probably a long rectangle extending away from the house. Definitely not a village haven with an orchard.

Through his career Thomas Church designed hundreds of such gardens in San Francisco and other parts of California, and developed an acute awareness of the requirements and limitations of confined areas. He combined his design skills with an understanding of human nature and appreciated that enforcing a certain plant for a garden would fail if it did not suit his clients' way of life.

He also learnt how to accommodate ambitious desires in a limited space. In *Gardens are for People* (1955) he said of one garden: 'Many people want – on a small lot – what used to be on an estate. This is a lot for 100 by 120 feet. The owners needed a two-car garage and a place for guests to park. They wanted a swimming pool, terraces to entertain lots of people, a vegetable garden, trees, and planting, and an arbor so they could eat outside in the shade. It all got there without seeming too crowded. The pool is raised because the land was high. Two sides have no path around the pool, which saves space. The garden is a series of outdoor rooms. The pool is decorated with tile collected in Spain.' The planting was concentrated in raised beds between the pool and terrace edges and the boundary fence. The neat arrangement of square-edged spaces and the changing levels from raised beds to pool, steps and terrace, provide an air of spaciousness that disguises the small area.

Many of Church's successes with small gardens came from a plan that focused on one major feature, as he described in the same book: 'It is important that a garden be built around a dominant idea. Do one thing well and let all others be subordinate to this

The concept of a series of garden rooms leading one to another was exemplified by Beatrix Farrand at Dumbarton Oaks, where this yew-hedged enclosure with its hip-roofed gazebo is part of a sequence.

(*Above*) Thomas Church often stressed the importance of orderliness in a small garden as illustrated by his immaculate design here. (*Opposite*) A small garden by John Brookes shows the effectiveness of foliage shapes and hard surfaces in a confined area.

idea. If it be a central grass plot surrounded by a flower border do not clutter the area with miscellaneous planting and garden ornament which will distract the eye and diminish the dramatic effect of the scale of the original conception.' In many of his gardens the central feature was a swimming pool, or perhaps a single mature tree around which the rest of the garden was designed in intimate detail. He used a wide range of patterns: straight paths and squares; flowerbeds or hedges making a diagonal across a garden's main axis; or circles and curving paths. And yet the precise arrangement of neat edges, boldly patterned paths and pool surrounds, and groups of plants in scale with each other and with the garden as a whole, ensured that the garden had a satisfying, orderly atmosphere.

In a confined space the choice of materials assumes an importance that is not relevant to a larger area where there is not the same regular use. Traditional and enticing though the idea may be, a grass lawn demands hours of mowing, edging and manicuring, and is often impractical. A hard surface can provide a more satisfactory, year-round alternative.

Church was acutely aware of this and used a variety of materials. John Brookes too skilfully uses gravel in confined spaces. Where informality is desired gravel is the ideal medium for the irregular placing of bold foliage plants as shown in his garden at Denmans. In the herb area gravel sweeps around strong groups of plants giving structure to the overall design and neatness that could not be achieved so easily with grass. Brookes' gravel designs are an important example of how small contemporary gardens have often encouraged designers to use new materials and satisfy the requirements of the owner, be they horticultural or social.

In a small area a random or cluttered style of gardening is unsettling. Too much detail can make a garden look smaller and, as Church said in the same book, 'if the eye sees too many things, it is confused and the sense of peace is obliterated.' Church understood the need for clarity. He added: 'To succeed in making a logical and intelligent plan which will produce the maximum in terms of use and beauty, one must have simplicity of layout, integrity in the use of plant and structural materials, and a sure sense of proportion and pleasing form.

'Whether your design is "formal" or "informal", curved or straight, symmetrical or free, or a combination of all, the important thing is that you end up with a functional plan and an artistic composition. It must have good proportion and proper scale and plants that have been chosen wisely and cared for affectionately.'

The minute attention to detail evident in both Lutyens's and Church's work is a hallmark of Preben Jackobsen's designs. In sympathy with Church's suggestion for one major feature, his garden at Stanmore was created around a rectangular swimming pool. Around it he concentrated on detail, be it the mixture of brick, paving or hard edges to borders, or the plant arrangements which were primarily chosen for shape more than flowers. The manner in which shallow rising steps flow into flower borders on corresponding levels cleverly makes the most of adding an upward element to the garden's strongly linear plan. This is also balanced by the arrangement of large natural boulders amongst the planting. A wooden pergola around two sides of the garden similarly adds a strong vertical element and an opportunity for planting.

(*Right*) The use of a focal point, such as the ever-visible white bench at Little Peacocks, is important in small-garden design. (*Far right*) In this design by Preben Jakobsen, rich foliage such as the deep green hostas softens the line of steps while climbing roses add a vertical element that is often important in a small garden.

Index

Page numbers in *italic* refer to illustrations

Acknowledgements

The publishers would like to thank the following for
supplying illustrations for this book:

Apertures of Arundel 102
Arcaid/Richard Bryant 29
AWG Album, *The Edwardian Garden* by David Ottewill,
  Yale University Press 52
John Brookes 103 (bottom left)
The British Architectural Library, Drawings, RIBA,
  London 58 (top left)
University of California, Berkeley, College of
  Environmental Design, Documents Collection 60 & 70
Colvin & Moggridge Associates 36, 85 & 87 (bottom)
Conde Nast 79
Stuart Cooper 74 & 120 (top)
Country Life Picture Library 54, 55 (bottom), 57 (right) &
  58 (bottom)
De Belder Archives 93
Dumbarton Oaks, Trustees for Harvard University 71
  (bottom)
Valerie Finnis 98
Fletcher Steele Archives 30 (left), 75, 76 (left), 78 (bottom)
Roger Foley 107
Felice Frankel 30 (right), 76 (right) & 78 (top)
Garden Picture Library 62 (Clay Perry) & 138 (top) (Clive
  Boursnell)
Grace Hall 67
Jerry Harpur 1, 6, 9, 26, 31, 34–5, 37, 46, 48–9, 50, 51, 63
  (top), 69, 71 (top), 91, 96, 103 (top), 103 (bottom right),
  114, 116, 121, 125, 126, 128, 130, 141, 149 (bottom),
  151, 152, 155 & 156
Peter Herbert, Gravetye Manor 14 (Please note that
  Gravetye Manor gardens are not open to the public)
Dr Hilary Grainger 64
Hulton Deutsch 57 (left)
Interior World/Fritz von der Schulenberg 38–9
Preben Jakobsen 44, 104 (John Cheesman) & 105
Sir Geoffrey Jellicoe 89 (top) (Heineman)
Nada Jennet 145
Andrew Lawson 10, 12 (bottom), 66, 113, 127 & 132–3
Mansel Collection 11
S & O Mathews 94
National Trust 20, 41 (Ian Shaw), 80, 81, 83, 84 (Andrew
  Lawson), 110 (Ian Shaw), 111 (Eric Crichton), 118 (Rob
  Matheson), 124–5 (Andrew Lawson), 138 (bottom), 148
  (Eric Crichton)
Clive Nichols 42, 73, 122, 123 & 140

Nigel Nicholson 34 (bottom), 82 (top)
Hugh Palmer 2, 8, 15, 23, 24, 33, 61, 65, 86, 87 (top), 88,
  92 (top), 93 (bottom left), 117, 132, 134, 136, 139, 142,
  146, 149 (top) & 154; Royal Horticultural Society,
  Lindley Library 12 (top), 16, 18 & 28; M C R Sandys
  Esquire 53
Harry Smith Collection 100 & 101 (top)
George Stewart/R W M & J M Monks, *The Edwardian
  Garden* by David Ottewill, Yale University Press 63
  (bottom)
Sutton Place Heritage Trust 92 (bottom right)
Oehme & van Sweden Associates 108 & 109 (left) James
  van Sweden) & 109 (bottom)
Volkmar Wentzel 106
Wildlife Matters 68 (top)
Steven Wooster 153
George Wright 99.

The black & white illustrations were taken from the
following:

The Art & Craft of Garden Making by Thomas Mawson 19,
  53, 55 (top), 56, 120 (bottom) & 135
Gardens For Small Country Houses by Gertrude Jekyll 21, 22,
  & 58 (top right)
Gardens Are For People by Thomas Church ©, 68 (bottom),
  115 & 132
The Guelph Lectures on Landscape Design by Sir Geoffrey
  Jellicoe 15 (bottom)
Lanning Roper and His Gardens by Jane Brown, © Mrs Anne
  Sidamon-Eristoff 101 (bottom)
Sissinghurst Castle Garden, National Trust booklet
  (Christine and Stuart Page) 82.

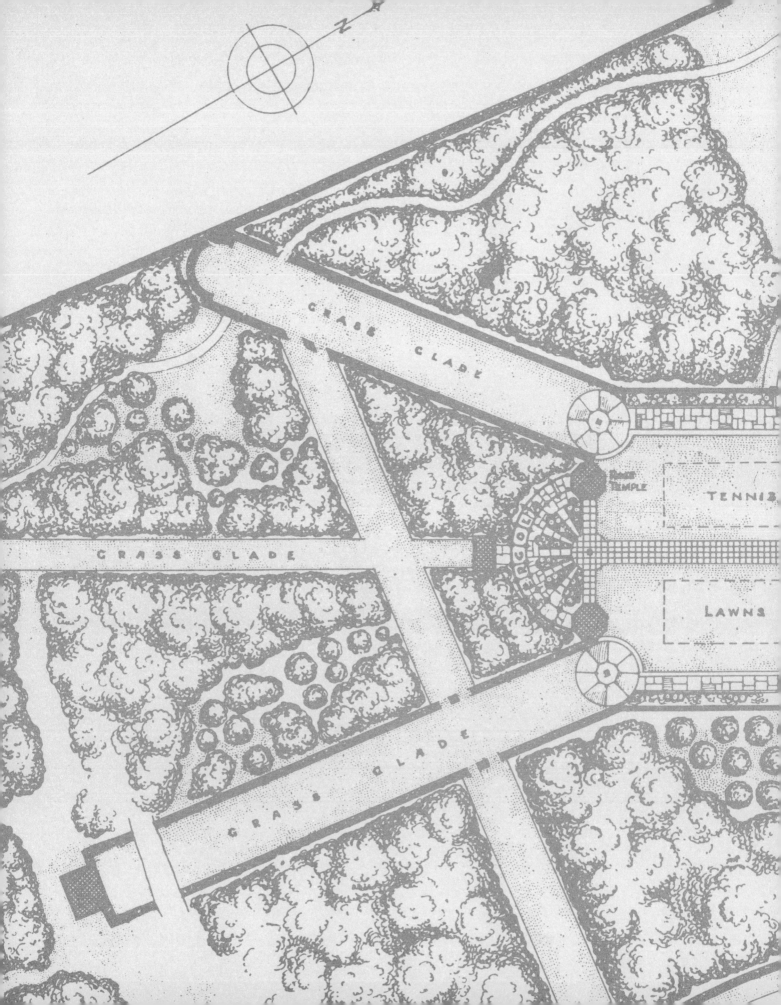

GRASS GLADE

GRASS GLADE

GRASS GLADE

TEMPLE

TENNIS

LAWNS